The Christian Table of Duties

A description of various estates and orders of Christians: Teachers, Hearers, Rulers, Subjects, Spouses, Parents, Children, Menservants and Maidservants, Masters and Mistresses, Young People, Widows, and then all men in general—what each one ought to do or leave undone in his vocation and estate.

Arranged and compiled in twelve different sermons
now published in a second, amended edition

by

Aegidius Hunnius,
Doctor of Holy Writ and Professor at Marburg in Hesse

Printed in Frankfurt am Main
by Johann Spiess, 1588

Translated by
Paul A. Rydecki

Repristination Press
Malone, Texas

A translation of the original title by Aegidius Hunnius: *Christliche Haußtafel. Das ist: Beschreibung allerley Stände und Orden der Christen, als da seind: Lehrer, Zuhörer, Obrigkeiten, Unterthanen, Eheleut, Eltern, Kinder, Knechte und Mägde, Herren und Frauwen, gemeine Jugend, Wittwen, und dann ins gemein alle Menschen, was jedem in seinem Beruff und Standt zuthun oder zulassen gebüre (1588).* Copyright 2013 by Paul A. Rydecki. Published by permission of the translator. No part of this publication may be reproduced, stored in a retrieval system, or transmitted in any form or by any means, electronic, mechanical, photocopying or otherwise without the prior written permission of Repristination Press.

Repristination Press
P.O. Box 173
Bynum, Texas 76631

repristinationpress.com

ISBN 1-891469-55-X

Table of Contents

Foreword to the Christian Reader 5
First Sermon: The Holy Preaching Office 9
Second Sermon: Parishioners, Hearers 25
Third Sermon: Secular Authorities 37
Fourth Sermon: Subjects in the Secular Realm 51
Fifth Sermon: Husbands and Wives 65
Sixth Sermon: Parents 79
Seventh Sermon: Children 93
Eighth Sermon: Menservants and Maidservants 107
Ninth Sermon: Masters and Mistresses 119
Tenth Sermon: Young People in General 129
Eleventh Sermon: Widows 139
Twelfth Sermon: All People in Common 149
Index 159

Foreword to the Christian Reader.

The whole of Christianity is essentially divided into two chief parts, which encompass everything necessary to prepare Christians for every good work. The first part is pure teaching and faith; the second, a holy, God-pleasing life.

Each is so intimately bound to the other that, where either faith or life goes astray from God's Word, the other, too, quickly becomes unproductive and entirely useless.

For example, when a person, led astray by false teaching, believes and thinks wrongly about God and His will, his life cannot please God, either, no matter how much it seems to glimmer and glisten as holy before the world. For what does not proceed from true faith is sin (Rom. 14). And without faith it is impossible for a man to please God (Heb. 11). This is why all Pharisees, monks, Anabaptists and others (who lack true faith and knowledge of God) are completely and utterly lost, in spite of having adopted the outward appearance of a respectable life.

On the other hand, when it becomes apparent that a man's life and conduct are defective, being marred by sins against conscience, for all that he may otherwise outwardly confess the pure doctrine and proclaim with the mouth, "I believe! I believe!," nevertheless, it is nothing but hypocrisy, a sounding brass, a clanging cymbal, a dead faith—indeed, a mere illusion of faith that has an appearance of godliness, but denies the power thereof through the futile works of darkness. Our Lord Jesus Christ speaks against this and preaches in Mat. 7: "Not everyone who says, 'Lord, Lord,' will enter the kingdom of heaven, but he who does the will of My Father in heaven." St. James also deals with this in the second chapter of his epistle and simply denies all power and effectiveness to such a worthless believer who is devoid of both Spirit and works. He dismisses them as hypocrites, as those who only claim to be Christians, but who experience no true blessedness in their life and works, regardless of how fervently they boast with their mouth that their teaching is pure and their faith genuine.

Therefore, since right doctrine and an upright life must, to a great extent, accompany one another if a person wishes to be known as a Christian in both deed and truth, one can readily understand how useful it is to have the "Christian Pedagogy," or Table of Duties (as we usually call it) appended to our holy, beloved Catechism.

For just as the Catechism, as a brief extract or outline of the Bible, contains in itself the whole doctrine introduced and revealed by God, setting forth what a person is to believe from God's Word in all articles of the Christian religion—through which also God the Lord accomplished much good among His elect before the present time in the midst of the dreadful darkness of the Papacy—so the Table of Duties molds the course of a man's life and sets forth how each one, in his own estate, office and vocation, is to act and behave.

Yes, the Ten Commandments also teach us what God requires of us men, but they speak almost entirely in general terms; they show what all men together and in common are obliged to do, in accordance with the immutable will of the Almighty.

The Table of Duties, on the other hand, narrows the scope somewhat and shows individually, specifically, and in particular to each one in his vocation what is proper or improper for him to do.

For since the estates on earth are different, there are also different tasks involved with each, in such a way that it would not at all be proper for anyone simply to do or perform them all. For that would be to reach into a foreign office, if the ministers of the government wanted to usurp and take for themselves the authority of the preaching ministry. No, each one should remain within the confines of his vocation, even as the particular lesson for each estate is accordingly laid out from God's Word, specifically and distinctly, in the Table of Duties, for the purpose of informing and instructing Christians, so that, with this pattern and these parameters, each one is able to carry out his duty, resulting in praise and honor for God in heaven, and in edification for men on earth.

While the Christian Table of Duties is already highly regarded, it must be held in even higher esteem for this reason, that it has been compiled, not from human philosophy or from the sayings of Socrates or of Cato or from the moral judgments of other intelligent heathens (who otherwise are rightly praised in their place), but it has been established only and alone by the testimonies and sayings of the Holy Spirit as a brief Christian book of ethics, so that whoever despises it, despises not man, but God, who has given His Holy Spirit among us, through whom, by means of the written prophetic and apostolic Word, He has given this as His holy commandment from heaven.

The holy Apostle Paul in particular is careful, when writing to his dear children in the faith[1] concerning the doctrine of the Gospel, to remind them now and again of the Table of Duties and to point out diligently what they are obliged to do on account of the divine ordinance and commandment. He does this especially in the fifth and sixth chapters of the Epistle to the Ephesians, the third chapter of Colossians, and the second, third, fifth and sixth chapters of his First Epistle to Timothy. Likewise, the second and third chapters of Titus give clear testimony concerning the manner in which the aforementioned various offices of Christendom are dealt with. Each person is given his own text, and a useful, salutary lesson is placed before his eyes. The Table of Duties is also drawn, in large part, from these chapters.

In addition to the admirable benefits already noted, the Table of Duties also serves us in this way: That one can undoubtedly conclude from the testimonies of the Spirit of God contained therein how each estate of Christendom has its sure, immovable foundation in the clear Word of God. This is useful in the face of the vexing attacks of the devil, who, as a sworn enemy of every good institution of God, seeks either to bring contempt on these estates, or to abolish them entirely, thus throwing men's

---
1 *Pfarrkinder*

consciences into confusion, as, for example, he impugns, diminishes, and, to some degree, even condemns the holy preaching office through the Schwenkfeldians, the estate of civil authority through the horde of Anabaptists, and marriage—especially the marriage of priests—through the Papists.

Against these enemies, the Christian Table of Duties supplies us with a shield and weapon from the Holy Spirit's arsenal and armory to put out these flaming darts of the evil one and his minions, and to make our hearts steadfast and secure by means of God's Word, even as, in this explanation of mine, I have already outlined and described both of the aforementioned benefits, according to the gift bestowed on me by the Lord.

Therefore, since I have explained this Christian Pedagogy or Table of Duties little by little over the years here in Marburg in a series of twelve different sermons, and since some have asked me to copy them down and to share them more broadly, I have finally decided to take up this task, arranging these sermons in such a way that they may serve to educate Christians and improve the lives, not only of those who sought them from me, but of many others as well.

I approach this task with the sincere prayer that God Almighty, through Christ His Son, would preserve unshaken till the end of the world the three chief estates of Christendom, namely, the Preaching Office, Civil Authority, and the Domestic Estate, against all the ranting and raging of Satan; and that He would awaken the hearts of each and every person so that we may all faithfully work in our vocation with the mina of the gifts that He has loaned to us, in order that the great household of the eternal, heavenly House Father may be extended, that a peaceful life may be led among us men in all blessedness and honor, but most of all, that the saving knowledge of Jesus Christ may be implanted more and more in us and ever preserved for our eternal welfare. Amen.

Submitted in Marburg, on the 18th of August, Anno Christi 1586.

Aegidius Hunnius

First Sermon on the Table of Duties: The Holy Preaching Office

To Bishops, Pastors and Preachers

A bishop must be irreproachable, the husband of one wife, vigilant, sober, of good behavior, hospitable, able to teach, as a steward of the house of God; not a wine guzzler, not violent, not pursuing dishonest trade; but patient, not a brawler, not covetous; one who rules his own house well, who has obedient children, with all respect. But if someone does not know how to rule his own house, how shall he take care of the church of God? Not a novice, lest he be puffed up with pride and fall into the condemnation of the devil, etc. 1 Timothy 3; Titus 1.

Beloved in the Lord Christ, now that we have given an explanation of the Catechism and brought it to completion[2], we will, with the help and attendance of God the Holy Spirit, set forth bit by bit the Christian Table of Duties that is appended to the Catechism. For here preachers and hearers, civil authorities and subjects, husbands and wives, parents and children, masters and mistresses, menservants and maidservants, and all men, both in general and individually, are reminded what each one ought to do or leave undone in his estate so that God the Lord may be served rightly and well according to His holy, divine will; and so that this temporal life may be lived in such quietness and peace that the eternal life of future blessedness may likewise be preserved along with it. Now, all the estates and offices in the world are divided into these three chief estates: First, the holy preaching office or ecclesiastical government. Second, the secular gov-

---

[2] Hunnius' *Christliche Hauβtafel* was originally published in conjunction with his sermons on the entirety of the Small Catechism.

ernment and the estate of civil authority. Third, the domestic estate or government of the house, where husbands and wives, parents, children and servants are found. We will begin with the ecclesiastical government, and, in the name of the Almighty, we will at this time discuss the holy preaching office in a simple way: its ministers, their office, doctrine, life and behavior, and how they are to conduct their ministry. In this sermon, we will seek to explain the office of an upright teacher, based not only on the previously read Word of St. Paul, but also on other testimonies of Holy Scripture. May our dear, merciful God deign to lend us His divine grace, so that our preaching may not only enter the ears, but that true Christian obedience may follow. Amen.

THE PREACHING OFFICE INSTITUTED BY GOD HIMSELF

Christians do not need anyone to prove to them that the preaching office was not established by men, but was instituted by God. It has been revealed to them by the holy, divine Word how in Paradise itself God conducted this office and preached the holy Law before the Fall, and, after the Fall, preached the dear Gospel concerning the woman's Seed, Jesus Christ. The office was then carried out in the ancient world through the patriarchs Adam, Seth, Enosh, Enoch the seventh from Adam, and through Noah, the preacher of righteousness. Likewise after the Flood it was propagated through Shem and all the other patriarchs that followed, both in the land of Canaan and in Egypt, until God raised up the great prophet Moses, who, at God's command, put down in writing that which had been preached orally in the congregation of the patriarchs. His books were preserved by means of the holy preaching office in the Levitical priesthood.

And when, in the course of time, the priests became either negligent in their office, or, rather, when they departed from the true worship of God, God raised up the prophets to the preaching office. They did not produce their prophecies from human will, but, as Peter testifies, they "spoke, being driven by the Holy Spirit" (2 Pet. 1). This office was thus preserved over time in the

Levitical priesthood and in the synagogues until the heavenly Teacher Jesus Christ was born into the world, who brought forth the eternal Gospel from the bosom of His Father and revealed it to us, and was not at all ashamed to teach and preach in the Jewish land in His very own Person. The heavenly Father also presented Him from heaven to us men as our only Master and Teacher and, in Mat. 3:17, earnestly commanded us to listen to Him, saying: "This is My beloved Son, with whom I am well pleased. You shall listen to Him." Afterwards, Christ sent His apostles into the world to proclaim the Gospel of the kingdom. They, in turn, called and ordained others after them to the preaching office, and they, in turn, called and ordained others after them, as the apostle writes to Titus in the first chapter: "For this reason I left you in Crete, that you might ordain bishops here and there in the cities." Thus—God be praised!—the office has been preserved by divine shelter and protection in the dear and precious Christian Church against all the ranting and raging of the world, the devil, and all the gates of hell, right up to our time. For this, we can never give sufficient thanks to the Almighty.

HOW HIGHLY ONE SHOULD ESTEEM THE PREACHING OFFICE

But how highly this estate is to be regarded must not be drawn only from the fact that it now announces what the Lord God and our Savior Christ Himself once preached, but also from the fact that God still to this day wants the word of the preacher to be viewed and regarded, not as the speech or thoughts of men, but as His very own Word, so long as it is stated in accord with the Holy Scriptures and in harmony with the faith. "He who hears you," says Christ, "hears Me. He who rejects you rejects Me" (Luke 10). Indeed, the apostle praises his Thessalonians for having accepted his preaching, not as the word of men, but (as it really was) as the Word of God (1 The. 2).

Therefore, Christ commended the Keys of the kingdom of heaven to His disciples and to those who would come after them, and He placed them in the holy preaching office of His Church.

Indeed, He says to Peter in Mat. 16: "All that you shall bind on earth shall also be bound in heaven. And whatever you shall loose on earth shall also be loosed in heaven." And what He here says to St. Peter, He repeats after His resurrection to all of His disciples in John 20 when He breathes on them and says: "Receive the Holy Spirit. To whomever you remit sins, they are remitted. And to whomever you retain them, they are retained." This is also the reason, dear friends, why preachers are called ambassadors, legates and angels of the LORD of hosts in Ecclesiastes 5 and Malachi 2, as those who have been dispatched to the human race from the eternal heavenly court of God, charged with revealing to men the whole will of God and announcing His counsel and intentions. Thus St. Paul writes in his Second Epistle to the Corinthians, chapter 5: "We are ambassadors in the stead of Christ, for God exhorts through us."

All this is said, not in order to glorify us ministers of the divine Word, but much more to highlight the worthiness and reputation of the office against the wanton blasphemers and godless mockers who think nothing of the preaching office, as in the ancient world, before the Flood, the Cainites did against Noah, the preacher of righteousness; as the Sodomites did against Lot; as the Israelites did against the prophets; and as the Jews did against Christ and His apostles. And at the end of the world, the tale will sadly be told in all too many cases how people mistook the word of the preachers for the drivel of men, how the vast majority pursued their temporal nourishment while viewing sermons and listening to sermons as merely a trivial distraction, devised by certain men only to maintain some degree of discipline among the people. The truth is that such people, deep down, do not believe that there is a God, or a future judgment, or eternal life, or eternal damnation. St. Peter prophesied about such mockers (2 Pet. 3) that there will be very many such people in the world in the last days, right before the coming of the Son of God. But blessed are they who do not walk, stand or sit where such mockers sit (Psalm 1) and who have neither a share nor anything to do with their mockery, but on the contrary, who recognize the dear preaching office as a special divine ordinance of God and as a salutary instrument through which God wants to work salvation among men, as it is written in Rom. 1: "I am not ashamed of the Gospel, for it is the power of God for salvation to everyone who believes." And again in 1 Cor. 1: "Since the world, through its wisdom, did not know God in His wisdom, it pleased God, through foolish preaching, to save those who believe in Him."

But the higher the holy preaching office is, the greater the care that is due, so that those who are placed into it by God should conduct themselves properly, irreproachably, and honestly in such a holy, lofty, worthy office. We will now hear more about this other part. For upright teachers should take special care to observe these two chief points: that they should teach and handle the Word of God purely, without any error, together with the Sacraments that are attached to it, and then that they should live according to it in a worthy and holy manner.

IN WHAT THE TEACHING OFFICE CONSISTS

In order to discover in what the teaching office consists, we must turn to St. Paul's words in 2 Timothy, chapter 4, where he writes thus to his disciple Timothy: "I hereby charge you before God and the Lord Jesus Christ, who is coming to judge the living and the dead in His appearance and in His kingdom: Preach the Word. Be attentive, whether in season or out of season. Rebuke, threaten, admonish, with all patience and teaching."

Thus a teacher is obliged to preach the Word, yet not his own word, not his own dreams or opinions, but only the Word of God, in such a way that nothing is added to it nor subtracted from it, as it is written in Jeremiah 23: "Surely I hear the false prophets preaching and prophesying in my name, saying: 'I had a dream! I had a dream!' When will the prophets stop prophesying falsehood and the imagination of their heart?" In summary, only God's Word should be preached, as Peter also admonishes: "Whoever speaks in the Church, let him speak as the Word of God." In this way, when the hearers are led only and alone to the salutary

Word of God, as to the fountains of Israel, they can build a sure foundation for their faith, so that they become certain of it, and they can remain steadfast in the hour of tribulation, where otherwise all human trumpery and human doctrine disappear and are consumed in the time of testing, even as the stubble is consumed by the fire (1 Cor. 3).

However, if one person should proclaim God's Word to another, then he must have a legitimate, regular call to do so, lest he be counted among those about whom it is written: "They ran, and I did not send them." In addition, whatever one person wishes to teach to another, he himself must first have studied and learned. He must have diligently read in the Holy Scripture and explored its interpretation and explanation. For the right opinion of the holy preaching office is not at all as the Anabaptists dream for themselves, who, although they are inexperienced in the Scriptures, nevertheless with great presumptuousness dare to undertake such a worthy work as this, in spite of being inexperienced in Holy Scripture. Their superintendents commonly go rushing off from the threshing floor or from some other job and prepare an inept sermon that has neither hands nor feet, in which nothing is treated in an orderly fashion. Instead, it takes off in a thousand different directions, and from then on it is considered by them to be pure holiness.

They cannot justify such a practice from the example of the holy apostles. For such an opinion was held concerning the prophets and apostles that they could preach a beneficial sermon to the people without much study because they were enlightened to do so in a special way by the Holy Spirit. Likewise, the Apostle Paul could also pursue his manual labor of making tents alongside the holy preaching office (Acts 18), even though he did this in order that he might not be a burden to the Corinthians, as he clearly shows (1 Cor. 9).

But not everyone is caught up into the third heaven, as Saint Paul was. Not everyone has such a Day of Pentecost as the apostles had, who in an instant were gifted with the ability to speak all the languages under heaven, and with the understanding of the Scriptures of the holy prophets. Instead, our Lord God has now permitted things to work in an ordinary manner and according to the rule that whoever wishes to teach must first learn. A teacher, therefore, should turn all his diligence to this end: that he should study well the Law of the Lord and His holy, saving Word; that he should build a firm foundation on it, so that not only he himself may sufficiently know the foundation of his faith and teaching, but also be apt to teach and able to impart the Word of God rightly, in order that he may be of benefit to others. Therefore, St. Paul admonishes Timothy in his First Epistle, chapter 4, that he should attend to reading, stir up in himself the gift that was given to him, and forego other employment. The admonition of Sirach also pertains to this as he says in chapter 39 of his book: "He who wants to learn the Scriptures cannot devote himself to other employment; whoever is to be taught must have nothing else to do. How can he concentrate on teaching when he has to plough, when he enjoys driving the oxen with the whip and spends his time with such labors and knows how to speak about nothing but oxen?" And shortly thereafter he says in the same chapter: "He who takes it upon himself to learn the Law of the Most High must seek out the wisdom of all the ancients and search in the prophets. He must take heed of the history of the renowned men and consider what they mean and what they teach. He must learn the spiritual language and exercise himself in deep parables."

Now, if he learns in this way and is regularly called to teach, then he should faithfully teach the Word of God, uncorrupted, without adding human doctrine or rules. Thus he will open up to his hearers the whole counsel of God, and hold nothing back that may serve for their edification and welfare. This is what St. Paul does in his earnest apostolic farewell to the elders in Ephesus. He boasts with a good and cheerful conscience that he has not withheld anything from them, but has proclaimed the whole counsel of God (Acts 20).

THE DISTINCTION THAT IS TO BE TAUGHT BETWEEN THE LAW AND THE GOSPEL

Furthermore, since the divine doctrine is divided into two chief parts, namely, Law and Gospel, which must be treated and urged with proper distinction in the Church of God, so it is also necessary for a teacher to point and direct all his sermons to the circumstance of his hearers in such a way that the ungodly are indeed terrified by the severe Law of God, but that the bruised consciences are encouraged and comforted by the sweet doctrine of the holy Gospel. The ungodly are to be shown their sin and are to be cautioned against it for God's sake. They must be threatened with God's judgment, wrath and displeasure over their sin. Yes, they must be threatened with temporal and eternal condemnation if they will not repent. And in this matter, no one should be spared, regardless of how important he may be. But in all this, Christian humility must be employed, as St. Paul had in mind when he said: "Rebuke, admonish, encourage with all patience and teaching." And again: "But a servant of the Lord should not be quarrelsome, but friendly toward everyone, able to teach. He should be able to bear the wicked with gentleness and rebuke those who are in opposition, if perhaps God may grant them repentance so that they may know the truth and be sobered up out of the snare of the devil, by whom they have been captured for his will" (2 Tim. 2). Here the Apostle has skillfully laid side by side both rebuke and Christian patience and gentleness, from which one may gather that such preaching of rebuke should not flow from human emotion or from one's own vengeance, but rather from a sincere desire to win the hearers and to warn them lest they perish eternally.

God requires such rebuking from those who preach. Indeed, this is His sincere and immutable will, as it is written: "Cry out confidently. Do not hold back. Lift up your voice like a trumpet and announce to My people their transgression, and to the house of Jacob their sin." [Isa. 58:1] And in Ezekiel 33: "O son of man, I have appointed you as a watchman over the house of Israel, that when you hear something from My mouth, you should warn them for My sake.

If I say to the wicked man, 'O wicked man, you must surely die!,' and you do not tell the wicked man to take warning because of his behavior, then the wicked man will surely die for his wicked behavior. But his blood I will require from your hand."

Thus a faithful teacher is obliged and duty-bound to threaten and to warn in the face of sins and all vice. And here he is to regard neither the pleasure nor the displeasure of men, but only the command of God. But just as vices in a man's life are to be rebuked with all earnestness, so also must error in a man's doctrine be rebuked just as earnestly, for since we are dealing with God's pure Word, no addition of human doctrine can be tolerated. For what do truth and lies have to do with one another? What fellowship exists between God's Word and error, between the pure, unadulterated dough of the Word and the yeast of human doctrine, error, falsehood and deception? "Let a prophet who has a dream preach his dream. But whoever has My Word, says the Lord, let him preach My Word rightly. What does chaff have to do with wheat? Is not My Word like a fire, and like a hammer that splits the rocks?" (Jer. 23).

Therefore, they are simply to be taken for hirelings, those who, when the wolf enters and does harm with false and impure doctrine, neither resist him nor drive him out, but instead wish to be seen as peace-loving men. They are to be considered hirelings when, in the face of error, they knowingly keep quiet on account of men and thus allow the error to enter in spades, through which irreparable harm is done to the congregation of God. With their unseasonable, imaginary, feigned love for peace, they demonstrate that they have no concern for God's Word or for the truth thereof, or for the eternal salvation of their flock, since they know that heresies and sects are counted in Galatians 5 among the damning sins, and nevertheless they knowingly put up with them in order to retain the favor of men. They are dumb dogs that cannot bark and are worthless for keeping watch. The wolf does whatever he pleases in the sheep pen of Christ. Therefore, if you wish to be a teacher of Christ Jesus or to become one in the future, then do not neglect this part of your office, namely, that you must rebuke and admonish. The Lord Christ hints at this in Matthew 5, where He speaks to His disciples in the parable of the salt: "You are the salt of the earth. If the salt becomes tasteless, what should one use for salt? It is no longer useful for anything but to be thrown out and trampled by men."

But just as the ministers of the Church of God must point out to the wicked his sin and transgression through the earnest preaching of repentance and admonition of the Law, so, in turn, they must be ready and willing to comfort the wounded, contrite conscience with the preaching of grace in the Holy Gospel, and, for the strengthening of such comfort in them, provide them with the truly salutary use of the Sacraments, which are added to the Word of the Gospel as a seal and grace of God. And so they must, in all things, keep watch over the flock over which the Holy Spirit has appointed them as shepherds and bishops, to feed the Church of God, which He purchased with His own blood (Acts 20). In doing this, as those who must one day give an answer and account to Jesus Christ, they will be careful never to neglect their children in the faith. In summary, faithful teachers are obliged ever to be prepared to teach, encourage, comfort, admonish and rebuke, and so to carry out the work of a true, evangelical preacher, as St. Paul requires of his disciple Timothy and of all God-fearing ministers of the divine Word.

HOW THE PREACHER'S LIFE IS TO BE CONDUCTED

But it is still not enough that you rightly and purely present the teaching of the truth to your hearers. It is likewise necessary that you yourself also practice what you preach. This, then, is the second chief part to which every teacher must give attention.

Indeed, the necessity of this can easily be seen from the previously read words of St. Paul. For in his description of the qualities of a true, faithful and esteemed teacher, the apostle summarizes the first part of the requirements of a bishop with a single phrase: "He must be able to teach." In contrast, he describes this second part in detail and at length, namely how the life of the preacher should be conducted. He sets forth, one after another, the virtues that ought to adorn a teacher, all to the end that doctrine and life should agree with one another in the spiritual shepherds and watchmen over the people of God.

Besides this, it is at once unseemly and wicked when a preacher teaches well, and yet lives in an evil manner. How can he preach against drunkenness with any benefit to his hearers if he himself is a drunk? Or how can he preach against greed or some other vice if he himself is flawed with the same things? Paul applies this directly to the supposed teachers among the Jewish people in Romans chapter 2: "You convince yourself that you are a guide for the blind, a light for those who are in darkness, an instructor of the foolish, a teacher of the simple. You have the form of knowledge and truth in the Law. Now you teach others, and you do not teach yourself. You preach that one should not steal, and you yourself are a thief. You say that one should not commit adultery, and you yourself are an adulterer. You abhor idols, and you yourself steal from God. You boast of the Law, and you profane God through transgression of the Law. For on account of you God's name is blasphemed among the Gentiles."

The scribes and Pharisees were such preachers at the time of Christ. They purported to be Rabbis in the Law, as those who had not only learned everything that was written therein, but had also fulfilled and kept it all. They taught others, but they themselves did not do what they taught. Christ rebukes them for this with all earnestness in Matthew 23 when He says to His disciples: "The scribes and Pharisees sit in Moses' seat. Whatever they tell you to observe, observe it and do it. But according to their works you should not do. They say it indeed, but they do not do it. They tie heavy, unbearable burdens and lay them on men's necks, but they themselves do not move it with a single finger." So when preachers are offensive in this way and worthy of rebuke in their lives, they do unspeakable damage. For what they build with one hand, they tear down again with the other. They offend the Church of God, for as the pastor is, so also are the parishioners. And "if the abbot casts the die, the convent begins to play." In other words, if preachers themselves lead a sinful, shameful life, then the hearers fail to guard themselves from the same sins. Instead, they think, "If my pastor or teacher really thought that coveting, drunkenness, sexual immorality, blaspheming God and other such things were so wrong, then he himself wouldn't do them." Thus the people become crude, secure and godless. The highly esteemed preaching office falls into disrepute. The most holy name of God is blasphemed on their account. And those for whom Christ died, those whom He so lovingly and dearly entrusted to the ministers of the Church—they are miserably led astray into all sins, even to their eternal destruction.

Such offensive behavior is even more burdensome to a preacher, because it offends, not just one or two individuals, not just ten or twenty, but a whole congregation. Christ says in Mat. 18: "Whoever offends one of the least of these who believe in Me, it would be better for him if a millstone were hung around his neck, and he were drowned in the deepest part of the sea. Woe to the world on account of offenses! Indeed, offenses must come, but woe to the man through whom it comes." If, then, the eternal woe and judgment comes upon him who offends only one person—dear God! How much greater must the judgment be for the offensive preachers who cause not just one, two or three, but a hundred or more people to fall all at once with their vices!

Therefore, we must constantly remember what it means to be a godly, faithful teacher and keep before our eyes this reading from St. Paul in 1 Timothy 3, where he clearly indicates how it is necessary for a teacher to behave without offense. This passage is now read from the Table of Duties, namely, that "a bishop must be irreproachable." Not, to be sure, as if he could be entirely irreproachable before God, nor as if he could actually please everyone, which is an impossible task. For people will always have something to find fault with in preachers, even if their life were as holy as that of John the Baptist. Indeed, the world was not even entirely content with the life of the Lord Christ and of His forerunner John (Luke 7), although it did not know of any good reason for which to rebuke them.

This is especially true, because God has not set angels in the holy preaching office, but men who still carry flesh and blood around with them, so that, accordingly, they have their faults and flaws and are not irreproachable before God, since no man is guiltless before Him. And so they must also pray no less than others, "Forgive us our debts." Nevertheless, a preacher should be irreproachable in this way, that no one can rightly blame him of the gross vices that St. Paul here enumerates. He should not be a wine guzzler, nor a brawler nor a striker, nor a usurer who pursues dishonest trade, nor quarrelsome, nor covetous, nor arrogant nor puffed up. Instead, he should lead a quiet, disciplined, chaste life, being a husband of one wife, says the apostle.

So the holy estate of matrimony is, in fact, permitted to preachers, contrary to the godless, antichristian ban of the despicable papacy, in which the marriage of priests is condemned. Indeed, the pope, together with his followers, have thus been revealed as the devil's teachers, since this most enlightened apostle clearly and manifestly predicts, in the fullness of the Spirit, such a ban of marriage in 1 Timothy 4, and condemns it as a doctrine of the devil. Here St. Paul permits a bishop to be the husband of one wife, so that he may live a disciplined and chaste life, avoiding sexual immorality and every kind of impurity. Yes, even his governing of his home should be proof of whether he is capable of governing the Church or not. Along with this, let the preacher also pay careful attention that he demonstrate the virtues that Paul enumerates, so that he may be moderate and sober in food and drink, virtuous and friendly in word and deed, hospitable and generous toward the poor and needy, and also toward those who are persecuted into poverty for the sake of the truth. Let his wife also be adorned with such virtues, that she may be a good example to the whole congregation. Let his children be obedient, being brought up in all godliness and respect. In summary, let him be an example to the whole flock entrusted to him, as St. Paul admonishes in 1 Timothy 4: "Be an example to the believers in word, in behavior, in love, in the Spirit, in faith, and in chastity." When teaching and life come together in such fine agreement, then the parishioners will soon follow suit and will be built up for every good work, not only through the teaching of the preacher, but also through his life and behavior, if he thus lives a life worthy of the Gospel, and if he himself puts into practice with his deeds what he teaches others from God's Word.

But since Satan remains the wretched enemy of the holy preaching office and undertakes to cause as much pain as possible to its ministers as those who are breaking apart his kingdom, there is hardly any virtue more essential for them than steadfast patience in the face of tribulation and adversity, so that, when the devil and the world rise up against them and at times even threaten them with death, they do not allow themselves to be driven away by any danger or tribulation from God and His holy Word, but instead suffer all things patiently, as well-fitted knights and soldiers of Jesus Christ (2 Tim. 2). This they do, considering that the same things also happened to their Lord Christ Himself and to His prophets and apostles. For, indeed, "the disciple is not above his Master, and the servant is not above his Lord. If they have persecuted Me," says Christ, "they will also persecute you" (John 15).

But along with this is the comfort that God accompanies them in every adversity, and that they will one day be rewarded handsomely in heaven, as the Son of God made known to His faithful minister in Rev. 3—to the angel, the teacher in Philadelphia: "Since you have kept the Word of my patience, I will also keep you from the hour of trial that is coming upon the whole circle of the world, to test those who live upon the earth. See, I am coming soon! Hold onto what you have, that no one may take your crown. Him who overcomes I will make a pillar in the temple of My God, and he will go out no more. And I will write on him the name of My God, and the name of the new Jerusalem, the city of My God that is coming down from heaven, from My God, and My new name. He who has ears, let him hear what the Spirit says to the churches."

The prophet Daniel also has in mind this glorious reward, as he speaks with these words in chapter 12 of his book: "But the teachers will shine as with the splendor of heaven, and those who lead many to righteousness, like the stars forever and ever." And likewise in 1 Peter 5: "I encourage the elders who are among you—I a fellow elder and witness of the sufferings that are in Christ and one who shares in the glory that is to be revealed: Feed the flock of Christ that is entrusted to you, and attend to it, not under compulsion, but willingly, not for the sake of shameful gain, but from the bottom of your hearts, not as those who lord it over the people. Be an example for the flock. Thus, when the chief Shepherd is revealed, you will receive the incorruptible crown of honor." The apostle Paul comforts himself again and again in all adversity with this aforementioned reward: "I have fought the good fight," he says in 2 Tim. 4. "I have finished the race. I have kept faith. Now there is laid up for me the crown of righteousness which the Lord, the righteous Judge, will award to me on that Day. And not to me alone, but also to all who love His appearing." May God—Father, Son and Holy Spirit—graciously grant this crown of glory to us also and crown us with it in His good time. Amen.

Second Sermon on the Table of Duties: Parishioners or Hearers

Taken from 1 Thessalonians chapter 5:
We ask you, dear brothers, to recognize those who work among you and are over you in the Lord and admonish you. Hold them even more dearly on account of their labor, and be at peace with them.

Dear Christians, we were reminded from the Table of Duties in the previous sermon about the preachers and ministers of the divine Word: their estate, office, doctrine and life; how they are to lead the way for the people and be an example for them. Now we will consider the hearers: how they, in turn, should be disposed toward these caretakers of their souls—their preachers and teachers—and toward the teachings and admonitions of their teachers. Moreover, we wish here to explain the passage read above from St. Paul, in order that we may understand the testimony of the Holy Spirit Himself as to what He would require of the hearers over against the caretakers of their souls.

This is what St. Paul says: "We ask you, dear brothers, to recognize those who work among you and are over you in the Lord and admonish you. Hold them even dearer on account of their labor, and be at peace with them." With these words, he commends and entrusts to them the teachers and ministers of the Word in the church of the Thessalonians. For it was the ministers who worked among them, preached the Word, instructed them in the confession of the Gospel, and were over them in doctrine and admonition. How, then, should the Thessalonians be disposed toward them? They should recognize this, he says. Understand what it is that you have in your teachers, what a great gift it is when God gives faithful, pure teachers to a congregation. And for this reason, you should hold them dear and esteem them highly. For even though they are poor, frail human beings, nevertheless you are to hold them dear on account of their labor, he says.

But the devil's ways were by no means unknown to the holy apostle Paul, who was aware that the devil applies all diligence to see how he might drive a wedge between preachers and hearers, so that offense is caused, divisions are fostered, and the course of the holy Gospel is notably hindered when the teachers themselves are always at loggerheads with their parishioners, fostering disunity. Therefore, in order that the evil foe may be driven back, he says, maintain peace with them, so that love and good faith may be preserved on all sides and the bond of unity remain undisturbed.

That is a brief summary of the meaning of the words of St. Paul, which contain and comprehend all that is required for hearers to render to their leaders. And what St. Paul once taught the Thessalonians should, of course, be applied to all churches, brought into use, and put into practice.

So, then, Christians are obliged to hold their teachers dear. For if we love our parents according to the flesh who gave us birth into this world, then we should naturally also hold them dear through whose ministry and preaching God has instilled in us not temporal, but eternal life, as St. Paul says: "In Christ Jesus I have fathered you through the Gospel" (1 Cor. 4). Therefore he praises his Galatians for this: "I am your witness that, if it had been possible, you would have torn out your eyes and given them to me" (Gal. 4). But along with such love, proper honor is also required, so that the hearers are indebted to their teachers for God's sake and for the sake of the high office that they bear and carry out. This is not said in any way as if we preachers were seeking honor for ourselves, but only in order that the hearers may be instructed from the Word of God itself as to what God the Almighty expects from Christian hearers in this regard. Sirach says in chapter 6: "Fear the Lord with all your heart, and hold His priests in due honor." St. Paul repeats this in 1 Timothy 5:

"The elders who lead well should be considered worthy of double honor, especially those who labor in the Word and in the teaching." Thus when he commends to the Philippians their apostle and caretaker of souls Epaphroditus, he writes that they should "receive him in the Lord with all joy and hold such people in honor." Likewise St. Paul testifies to his children in the faith in Galatians 4 that they received him as an angel of God, as Jesus Christ Himself.

This should be noted well by those who hate, oppose, profane, abuse and blaspheme the custodians of their own souls, where they can or may speak poorly of them only for this reason, that they zealously rebuke their vices. Such people are not worthy to be called Christians. If you strayed into a dense, dark forest, wouldn't you thank the one who brought you back onto the road? Wouldn't you be grateful to the one who pulled you out of a lake or who rescued you from a fire? But what else do preachers do when they rebuke your sins, but to turn you from the path of error that leads to hell and lead you onto the right road of life so that you escape the eternal fire of hell? Therefore, you ought to know even more how to thank those who, as dear fathers, warn you sternly in the face of your temporal and eternal destruction.

But it is the devil's work and influence when hearers commonly show the most remarkable ingratitude for the tremendous blessing of these custodians of their souls. There have always been many of these mangy sheep in the Church, as the prophets, Christ, and the apostles experienced all too often when they preached on the earth. The prophet Isaiah (Isa. 30) describes his flock as a sinful people and as rebellious children who were angry with him because he preached the Law of God sharply to them and rebuked their sin and refused to preach gently to such godless scoffers. Jeremiah complains about his hearers that they tried to take away his body and life and desired to smite him to death with their tongues. Micah speaks of his own people: "If I were a spirit of error and a preacher of lies and I taught them how they should get drunk and indulge themselves, that is just the preacher for this people" (Micah 2). It was the same for the holy prophet Ezekiel: "Your people," God says to Ezekiel, "are speaking against you behind the walls and under the doorways of their houses, and each one says to the next, 'Come, friend, and let us hear what the Lord says!' And they will come to you in the assembly and sit before you as My people, and they will hear your words, but will not act according to them. Instead, they will voice their agreement with you, and yet will go on living according to their covetousness. And behold, you must be their little song that they will gladly sing and play" (Ezekiel 33).

Such scoffers should know that they are not only dealing with men, but with God, who will not permit His servants to be despised. "He who hears you, hears Me. He who despises you despises Me," says Christ (Luke 10). For as little as a lord can allow his legate to be taunted or mocked, so little—yes, much less—can God suffer His messengers and ambassadors (as Paul calls them) to be despised. For this reason, He sometimes also shows His judgment on such despisers. Korah, Dathan and Abiram rebelled against their legitimate teachers, Moses and Aaron. They spoke hatefully about them before the people. They despised and blasphemed them. But God revealed His judgment, wrath and punishment from heaven against these perpetrators. Indeed, Dathan and Abiram were swallowed alive by the earth, while Korah, together with his followers, had to be consumed and wiped out by fire, with all their belongings (Num. 16). So also when the vile knaves at Bethel called out to the prophet Elisha in mockery and spite, "Baldhead, come up! Baldhead, come up!", they had to be eaten up by bears (2 Kings 2). This, then, is the second thing God requires. He would have His servants held in honor by their parishioners.

Now, where proper love exists among the hearers and due honor for their preachers is found, there one will also certainly find the third thing that they owe their preachers, namely, obedience in the Church—that they follow their teaching, admonition, instruction and warning. This is required of true Christians no less than the other two requirements. The Holy Spirit speaks about this in Hebrews 13 and commands with these words: "Obey your teachers and follow them. For they watch over your souls as those who must give an account for it—so that they do it with joy and not with a heavy heart." For when preachers teach, encourage, admonish or rebuke, they do not do it in their own name; they do it in the stead of God, who has solemnly charged them with it. Indeed, it is properly the office of the Holy Spirit, as we have clearly demonstrated in the previous sermon. For this reason, Christ speaks about the teaching office of the apostles: The Holy Spirit will do it. The Holy Spirit will carry out this office of yours (although He will do it through you and those who come after you). The Holy Spirit will rebuke the world because of sins, because of righteousness, and because of judgment" (John 16). But if anyone despises this and is disobedient and contentious, he despises not men (says Paul in 1 The. 4), but God, who has given His Holy Spirit to this high office of preaching and teaching.

The ancient unbelieving world, before the Flood, also imagined that it was dealing only with Noah when they were disobedient to his preaching. But the Lord says something quite different in Genesis 6: "Men will no longer be permitted to contend with My Spirit." Since the people of Israel opposed the prophets and refused to follow their preaching, the Lord most assuredly called them to account for such disobedience, by which they sinned against God Himself and against His divine majesty, as Isaiah explains (ch. 46), so that they embittered His Holy Spirit and filled Him with indignation. Stephen says to the Jews in Acts 7: "You stiff-necked and uncircumcised of heart and ears! You always strive against the Holy Spirit. As did your fathers, so also do you." With these words he wants to lead them to recognize that, even though they (the Jews) imagined that they were striving solely against the apostles as men when they hostilely persecuted them, nevertheless God views their persecution much differently. He calls it "striving against the Holy Spirit."

Therefore, whoever hears the word of the preachers and still does not follow it, he hears it for judgment and as a testimony against himself, that his condemnation is increased by such disobedience and that his judgment will be that much worse. Indeed, it would be better for him if he were an unbelieving pagan instead of such a perverse Christian who bears the name of a Christian and yet denies the power of the Christian faith with his wicked deeds, disobedience and insubordination. We hear at times how harshly the prophets cry out against such disobedient hearers. "Oh, with whom shall I speak," says Jeremiah in chapter 6, "that he would actually listen? But their ears are uncircumcised; they cannot hear. Behold, they consider the Word of the Lord to be a joke and do not desire it. Therefore I am so full of the fury of the Lord that I cannot bear it." In chapter 44, they say in his presence: "According to the word that you speak to us in the name of the Lord we will not do, but according to the word that proceeds from our own mouth."

Good-hearted preachers are troubled by such disobedience. The Holy Spirit in them is grieved, so that they carry out their office with a heavy heart. This, according to the word of the apostle, is not good for the parishioners. For we hear daily how God punishes this sin every time: in the terrifying examples of the ancient world, the Sodomites, the Jewish people, and also other nations, peoples and kingdoms from whom God took away His holy Word, which they refused to follow and obey. In its place, He sent them a powerful error, so that they had to perish in it for time and for eternity, body and soul. Surely this should serve as a stern and powerful sermon for us to guard ourselves from similar disobedience against the most holy Word of God.

In the fourth place, even if the hearers notice faults, defects and deficiencies in their preachers, they should not become angered by it, since God has not placed angels in the holy preaching office, but men. There is, of course, a big difference between public, gross vices and common human weakness, even as there is between error in doctrine and sins in life. For if a preacher is tainted with gross vices and yet at the same time teaches correctly, Christian hearers should still follow his teaching, as long as it is presented undefiled. They should leave it to God to judge the offensive life of their teacher (assuming he is not removed from office by those who have authority to do so). For although the sinful life of the preacher in a congregation is extremely harmful, and many people are confirmed in their sin by it and hindered from true repentance and conversion, nevertheless the sermon remains no less a salutary instrument through which God wishes to work powerfully and effectively in those who receive it with believing hearts and who follow it in Christian obedience. Indeed, a teacher can certainly preach another toward salvation, while he himself is cursed and condemned, as is clearly written in 1 Cor. 9. However, especially when one does not even observe gross sin and vice in a preacher, but only common human defects and faults, then it is the right and Christian thing to do for godly hearers to bear with them patiently and to recognize that their preachers are also human beings who must daily ask others for the forgiveness of sins and who must sing the *Miserere*[3] together with David and all the saints. In all of this, however, the office should and must be upheld in its proper dignity. For the office does not belong to the individuals who carry out the ministry externally, but it is and remains the work of God and the office of the Holy Spirit (2 Cor. 3).

In the fifth place, parishioners are obliged to support their souls' custodians and the ministers of the Word of God with the proper necessities of life. For in the Old Testament God ordained that the priests and Levites should receive their living from the offerings and tithes that the rest of the Israelites were to give annually, as described especially in Numbers 18. And that which was thus given to the priests and Levites was designated by the Scripture as consecrated to the Lord Himself. If anyone held anything back from them or, contrary to God's command, failed to pay their dues, he was considered to have robbed God. Therefore, God in various places (e.g., Deu. 14, 18, 26) commands the Israelites in the Law that they should most certainly not forget the Levites in the land. And the wise teacher Sirach issues a warning in this regard to all pious, God-fearing Israelites: "Fear the Lord," he says, "and honor the priests, and give them their portion, as you are commanded, from the firstfruits and the guilt offerings

---

3 "Have mercy upon us!"

and heave offerings and whatever else is consecrated for the offering, and every kind of holy firstfruits" (Sirach 7).

But lest someone should claim that this was only necessary for the people of Israel, while now in the New Testament, with the abolition of the Levitical priesthood, there is a different intent, that each preacher should provide for himself with the work of his hands, as the Anabaptists rave and pretend, we must ponder well what the Holy Spirit has ordained in this matter under the Gospel in the kingdom of Christ. "Who ever embarks on a journey at his own expense?" says Paul in 1 Cor. 9. "Who plants a vineyard and does not eat of its fruit? Or who tends a flock and drinks not of the milk of the flocks? But am I saying this in a human manner? Does not the Law also say the same thing? For it is written in the Law of Moses: 'You shall not muzzle the ox while it threshes.' Is God concerned about oxen? Or does he not say this rather for our sake? Indeed, it is written for our sake. For he who plows should plow with hope, and he who threshes should thresh with hope that he will share in his hope. If we sow spiritual things for you, is it a great thing if we reap physical things from you? But if others share in this right over you, why should we not share in it much more?" And soon after the Apostle writes: "Do you not know that those who make the offerings eat of the offering? And those who attend to the altar enjoy of the altar? Thus also the Lord has commanded that those who preach the Gospel should receive their living from the Gospel, etc."

With these words, St. Paul makes it quite clear that it is required of hearers that they provide their souls' custodians and the ministers of the dear Gospel with the necessities of life. Indeed, he (the apostle) himself had the right to receive a salary from the Corinthians. But for the sake of a good cause, he did not wish to make use of his right.

But what Christ means when He says, "Freely you have received it. Freely give it also," is revealed from the text in Matthew, that this is to be understood concerning the working of miracles with which He gifted His apostles at that time in order to confirm the doctrine of the Gospel. For thus says Christ Himself in that place: "Heal the sick; cleanse the lepers; raise the dead; drive out the devils. Freely you have received it. Freely give it." Thus the dear apostles were not to charge any money for these miracles of theirs. Likewise the holy prophet Elisha refused to take anything whatsoever from Naaman, the Syrian commander, after healing him of leprosy through a divine miracle (2 Kings 5). Naturally we also grant that one should not practice simony with the dear Gospel, with the Absolution or forgiveness of sins, and with other such things. Nor should one sell such spiritual goods and gifts which God has been pleased to give us by grace, as the Antichrist in Rome has done, together with his followers, turning the remission or forgiveness of sins and other things into a scam and a shameful business in all of Christendom. For in doing this he has powerfully fulfilled St. Peter's prophecy (2 Pet. 2) as well as John's prophecy (Rev. 17 and 18) in himself and his entire horde.

But Christ did not intend with the aforementioned words that a preacher should not receive any salary for the toil and labor that he expends in carrying out his office, since this would not only contradict the incontrovertible testimony of St. Paul cited earlier, but it would also be contrary to Christ's own words, as He says even in the same chapter (Mat. 10): "A worker is worthy of his wages." St. Paul wrote the same thing to the Galatians in chapter 6: "Whoever receives instruction in the Word should share in every good thing with him who instructs him." For according to this, the holy preaching office must be performed in such a way that, when it is carried out rightly, one cannot hold another job (as we clearly demonstrated from the Holy Scriptures in the previous sermon). But the preachers, with their wives and children, cannot live on air, can they?, and without physical necessities and proper support. In addition to the command of God which we just heard, reason itself dictates that their proper support should and must be provided. Surely everyone should be all the more willing to do this, since, through their salutary ministry, God offers and distributes heavenly treasures and an incorruptible kingdom to men. What, indeed, is the temporal compared to the eternal? And what are the spiritual things which true preachers sow in their parishioners compared to the physical things which they, in turn, reap from their parishioners? Nothing at all! Competent Christians should be able to distinguish these things for themselves.

All of this is said for this reason, not to strengthen those who refuse to be satisfied with any salary—even a very honorable one—and serve more for the sake of their belly and shameful gain than from a sincere heart, but in order that Christians may hear what God Himself in heaven would require of hearers in this regard over against their teachers who have been set before them. Previously, under the papacy, the monks and Mass-priests were willingly and richly compensated, although Christendom wasn't improved a hair's breadth by any of them, but was instead miserably and shamefully defrauded and led astray by their idolatry and hypocrisy. But now, after God has again been pleased to restore to us His true divine service, people think that whatever is given to the ministers of the Gospel is simply wasted. As a result, when people are obliged to hand them some of the tithes or other things, they do it begrudgingly and often with a great deal of self-interest. What a wretched ingratitude toward the precious, heavenly treasure of the holy, saving Gospel! God will not let it go unpunished.

Therefore, in those churches where it is so arranged that the congregation must give a salary to their ministers of the Word, godly Christians should, from a willing heart, in accord with the apostolic admonition they have heard, share with those from whom they have received instruction in the Word (Gal. 6). They should also consider the promise of Christ in Mat. 10, who, as He was sending out His disciples into the Jewish territories to preach the Gospel of the kingdom without money and without purse, made them a glorious promise, that they would be given lodging, food and drink. "Whoever receives you receives Me. And whoever receives Me receives Him who sent Me. Whoever receives a prophet in a prophet's name will receive a prophet's reward. Whoever receives a righteous man in a righteous man's name will receive a righteous man's reward. And whoever gives a drink to one of the least of these with even a cup of cold water in a disciple's name—truly I say to you, he will not remain without a reward."

But in those places where the churches for a long time now have been reticent to provide any benefits and stipends beyond the bare necessities of life because the parishioners have grown weary of having to compensate their preacher from their own pockets, they should see to it that, having seen fit to give them nothing additional, they do not also withhold from them any of their legitimate compensation and salary. For the number is not few of those who scrape together and horde whatever spiritual goods and churchly benefits they can for themselves. But what they gain from this is evident, and experience prevails. For such spiritual goods eat away at their other goods, so that they become impoverished by God's righteous judgment. They carry around a gnawing worm in their heart and must ever be aware of God's wrath and displeasure with a fearful heart.

Let this, then, suffice concerning the office of Christian hearers and parishioners—in what manner and measure they are to be minded toward the faithful, dear custodians of their souls, pastor and preachers, namely, that they should love and honor them, be obedient to their word and follow their teaching, and even walk in their footsteps, assuming that they are leading a godly, holy life; and that they should give them what they are obliged to give them and, in all their ways, behave in such a way that they are a tribute to their preachers, as St. Paul writes about his Thessalonians: "Who is our hope or joy or crown? Is it not you before the coming of our Lord Jesus Christ? Indeed, you are our tribute and our joy."

May the Almighty God and Father of our Lord Jesus Christ accompany us paternally with His Holy Spirit, so that preachers and parishioners show themselves to be blameless in every aspect of their office, so that it may be carried out in a manner worthy of the holy Gospel of God, so that the name of God may be hallowed among us, His kingdom extended among the human race, the course of His eternal saving Word furthered, the Church of God planted thereby, and much fruit produced for the kingdom of our Lord Jesus Christ, in order that we may know Him from His holy Word and praise, honor and glorify Him eternally, together with all the elect. Amen.

Third Sermon: Secular Authorities

Let each one be subject to the authorities that have power over him. For there is no authority except from God. But where authority exists, it has been ordained by God. Whoever opposes the authority rebels against the ordinance of God. But those who rebel will receive judgment upon themselves, for he does not bear the sword in vain. He is God's minister, an avenger for punishment over those who do evil (Romans 13).

In the introduction to our treatment of the Table of Duties, we identified three estates that embrace all the others; namely, the holy preaching office, secular government, and domestic government. First we explained what the preaching office is, how teachers are to behave in it in every respect; how hearers are to be minded toward it, toward their pastors and teachers. Now we come to the second estate of secular authority here on earth. We wish at this time to explain what the office and vocation of secular authorities is, what they should do and leave undone, so that they may serve God rightly and do justice to their office.

But first of all, one finds people who criticize and reject this estate as being unchristian, as if one could not serve or please God in such a profession. The deceitful Anabaptists are among them. They would happily be free of the authorities, as they practiced and attempted in the Peasants' Revolt and in their astonishing, devilish behavior in Münster where they would have gladly slaughtered all the princes so that they could have lived, behaved and done as they pleased. In particular they claim that, although this estate was permitted in the Old Testament, nevertheless it now has a different intent in the kingdom of Christ.

But in order that both authorities and subjects may have a faithful description of their respective estates, we must go to the foundation and prove from God's Word that God indeed declares this estate to be well-pleasing to Him. The authorities, of course, need such a description so that they may be assured in their conscience that their estate is pleasing to God. But the subjects need it so that they know how they are to view this estate and what they owe to their authorities, which have been established by God.

In the first place, we have the Lord God Himself as the incontrovertible witness, who gives His own name to the secular authorities on account of the office that has been entrusted to them: that they should be called gods, as noted in Exodus 21 and 22, the 82nd Psalm of David, and John 7. Now, if secular authority were an unchristian, heathen estate, then surely God would never have graced it with His name. It is also a matter of record that many notable saints of God lived in this estate and were acceptable to the Lord while serving in it. Job was a prince in his country, as is evident from chapter 29 of his book; Joseph in Egypt; Moses, a ruler of the people of Israel, and Joshua after him. Likewise Barak, Gideon, Jephtha, Samson, and Samuel were judges in the land, were pleasing to God, and, through faith, defeated kingdoms, worked righteousness, and obtained the promise (Hebrews 11). Thus David, Solomon, Jehoshaphat, Hezekiah, Josiah, Daniel, Mordechai and others were either kings, or were given a role in the government and included among the authorities, and yet their estate neither hindered them in their salvation nor brought any shame upon them.

The Anabaptists, however, have no basis at all for their claim that, while this estate may well have been praised in the Old Testament, it has now been abolished by Christ. For if Christ had done away with the office of secular authority, His apostle surely would not have praised this estate so highly. And yet concerning the authorities in his day (obviously in the New Testament era), he confesses in the words read before, using various illustrations, that the authorities are an ordinance of God, ordained and established by God to such a degree that, whoever rebels against them rebels against God Himself in heaven and will not go unpunished. Also, if the Son of God had wanted to do away with this estate, then He and His apostle would have warned those individuals away from it who were in it, if they otherwise had wanted to be acknowledged as Christians. Now, when a centurion asked the Lord Christ in Matthew 8 to help his servant, Christ testified concerning him that he had such a faith the likes of which He had not found in Israel. He thus allows him to pass for a true Christian, and yet allows him to remain in the estate of secular authority. He says not a word about it—that he couldn't be both a Christian and a centurion. The soldiers (who also belong to this secular estate) came to John the Baptist in Luke 3, asking what they should do so that they may lead a God-pleasing life. John doesn't say a single word to them about needing to abandon their estate if they want to serve and please God. Instead, he lets them remain in their vocation and gives them only this teaching: they should not do harm or wrong to anyone, and they should be satisfied with their wages. Since he leaves them with their wages, he obviously leaves them also with their office on account of which the wages were paid to them. Thus also Peter simply allowed Cornelius the centurion to remain in his estate (which belonged to the civil realm), in spite of the fact that Peter had been sent to him by God to give him a full account of how he might be saved.

But if St. Peter had shared the understanding of the Anabaptists, he would have immediately said to him: "You must abandon your order; you cannot be saved if you remain a centurion." But Peter said no such thing. So also St. Paul did not command the proconsul at Paphos, Sergius Paulus, to abandon his vocation after he had believed the word of the Gospel that was preached to him, but allowed him to remain a proconsul, and thus a secular authority. Indeed, he let him pass for a believing Christian. From all this it follows irrefutably that secular authority is a good, unobjectionable estate and ordinance, and that the Anabaptists are being driven by the evil foe to rebel against this ordinance of God, to despise the government and to blaspheme the dignitaries, as Peter foretold of such people (2 Pet. 2).

In the second place, let us consider what the office of the state is. Here we again find people who define the office of the state much too narrowly, restricting it only to secular matters, as if it had nothing at all to do with religion and worship, as the papists claim, forbidding the authorities to read the Bible, since they have not been consecrated for the preaching office. But this is a grave misunderstanding on the part of the papists. For it is not the slightest part of the office of Christian rulers that, in presiding over the one, right, true worship in good faith and with due diligence, they should allow false worship, error, or seductive teaching to creep into the Church. Now, if the authority is to preside over the true worship and give no place to the false, impure worship, then he himself must also know from God's Word how to distinguish between true and false worship. Therefore, Christian rulers—whether at high level or low level—cannot and should not exempt themselves from spiritual matters, as the papists teach. In Deuteronomy 17 the Lord says: "When the king sits on the throne of his kingdom, he shall take a copy of this Law from the priests and Levites and have it written in a book that shall be near him. He should be reading in it throughout his whole life so that he may learn to fear the Lord his God, that he may keep all His Words of this Law and these statutes, that he may act according to them."

What could ever be said more clearly to demonstrate that the authorities, too, should receive their copies of the Holy Bible and should read it at all times? The aforementioned godly kings of Judah also did this, especially Josiah, who had his scribe or secretary Shaphan read to him the Book of the Law that was found in the temple. Far from being scolded for this, he is highly praised for hearing the words of the Book, for being stirred in his heart over it and for humbling himself before the Lord his God. Therefore, it was a particularly demonic attack against God's Word for the pope to forbid the governors, rulers and authorities to read the Bible. Indeed, this antichristian ban had this particular aim, that princes and lords should not be aware of the error, idolatry, horror and hypocrisy with which the pope and his spiritual horde had filled the Church of God and submerged it as with a destructive flood. For if they had permitted the authorities to read the holy Bible, they surely could have expected that all their deception would thus be exposed to the light of day. Therefore, we must give thanks to God, who has now brought it about that godly rulers again receive the dear Bible, together with the pure, unadulterated worship, and in this way they prove themselves to be Christian authorities who not only preside over the second table of the holy Ten Commandments, but also over the first, which properly deals with faith, religion and worship.

The second part of the office of the state belongs properly to secular matters, namely, that laws, justice, righteousness, and good policy be maintained, in conjunction with an honorable, calm, quiet and peaceful life among the subjects; that the innocent and godly be protected and aided by the law; but that the wantonness, wickedness and trespasses of the godless be put to an end.

Thus the authorities must, first of all, be gracious toward the godly, especially the poor and the oppressed. They must gladly give them a hearing, permitting their cases to come before them, and granting a gracious response and ruling that they may receive aid and support. Indeed, this is what Paul says: "The authority is ordained for the benefit of the godly." The wise and holy teacher Sirach explains it this way in chapter 4: "Give ear to the poor gladly, and answer him in a friendly and gentle manner. Deliver him who suffers harm from the one who does him wrong, and be not afraid when you must render judgment. Be like a father to the fatherless, and like a husband to their mother. So you will be like a son of the Most High, and He will love you more dearly than your mother does."

Solomon praises this virtue in great men in the 16th chapter of his Proverbs: "When the countenance of the king is friendly, there is life; and his grace is like the evening rain." And again in chapter 19: "The grace of the king is like dew on the grass." Likewise, the dear, pious Job caused the heart of the widows to rejoice after they were oppressed by their adversaries (Job 29).

But on the other side, a serious threat is also required against the disobedient, godless sinners, and transgressors of good law and order. Therefore, St. Paul says: "If you do evil, then be afraid. For he does not bear the sword in vain. He is God's servant, an avenger for punishment over him who does evil."

By means of such a threat, good policy and government are preserved and many an evil man is thwarted. "A wise ruler is strict," says Sirach. And "where there is prudent government, things are well-ordered" (Sirach 10). "A king or ruler who sits on his throne to judge scatters all wickedness with his eyes" (Pro. 20). David offers himself as an example of this, saying: "I hate the transgressor; a perverse heart must depart from me. I suffer not the wicked man who secretly defames his neighbor; I destroy him. I cannot stand him who has haughty gestures and a proud heart" (Psalm 101). And soon after: "Liars do not prosper with me; I quickly destroy all the wicked in the land, that I may uproot all evildoers from the city of God."

All God-fearing rulers surely have this same attitude, that they are hostile to all ungodly behavior, sin and vice, such as blasphemy against God, despising the divine Word, disobedience, quarrelling and enmity, murder, prostitution, adultery, drunkenness, theft, extortion, lies and false testimony, and whatever else is condemned and forbidden in God's Ten Commandments. All of these things should be earnestly punished, in accord with the transgression. And in order that such punishment may appear all the more honorable and have all the more effect, the authorities themselves should also avoid and flee from these vices in their life and conduct. They should let absolutely nothing hinder them from basic justice, both protecting the godly and punishing the wicked. But they should let the righteous man go about his business freely and unhindered, without any partiality.

This is what God repeatedly ordered the judges and rulers to do through Moses and the prophets, especially when He commands in Exodus 23: "Stay far away from false matters. You shall not strangle the innocent and the righteous, for I will not permit the wicked to be justified." And in Deuteronomy 16: "You shall not pervert justice, and you shall not show partiality nor take a bribe, for a bribe makes the wise blind and twists the matters of the righteous. Whatever is right, that you shall follow, so that you may live and inherit the land that the Lord your God will give you." This is repeated in Isaiah 1: "'Pursue justice,' says the Lord. 'Help the oppressed, do justice to the fatherless, and plead the case of the widows.'"

All secular government should certainly take this earnest commandment of God to heart. For it surely does not have supreme authority in such a high office to pursue its own pleasure according to human desire and will. But the government is God's minister; it has its specific instructions and must be conscious of what the supreme Lord and Judge of all the earth prescribes and demands of it.

For this reason, where the authorities truly fear God and keep His Word and command before their eyes, let them strive with the utmost diligence to carry out the instructions given to them, so that everyone may experience justice as the sword entrusted to the authorities is used to protect the godly, but to bring vengeance and punishment on the wicked. This is how Job behaved. He is praised for being altogether God-fearing and for shunning evil. He says this in the 29th chapter of his book: "I delivered the poor who cried out, and the fatherless who had no helper. The blessing of him who was about to perish came upon me, and I gladdened the heart of the widows. Righteousness was my garment that I put on as a cloak, and justice was my royal hat. I was the blind man's eye and the lame man's foot. I was a father to the poor, and if I didn't know a matter, I investigated it. I broke the fangs of the unrighteous and tore the prey from between his teeth."

Such faithfulness and diligence in this all-important office God will not allow to go unrewarded. For "through righteousness, godliness and truth will the king's throne be established" (Pro. 16 and 20). Josiah presided over justice and righteousness, and it went well with him. He gave justice to the poor and needy, and it went well with him (Jer. 22). Indeed, history testifies to the fact that God has at times caused the government of the heathen to arise and prosper when they pursued righteousness from the light of natural law, as the example of the ancient Romans demonstrates.

But what can or could be more wicked than when he who is the first to suppress justice is nevertheless entrusted by God with managing it? Sirach explains how evil this is by means of a parable in chapter 20 of his Wisdom: "He who exercises violence in the judgment is like a house-master who defiles a virgin whom he is to be protecting." God in heaven is utterly opposed to this, since, as it is written: "He who justifies the wicked and condemns the righteous—both are an abomination to the Lord." Therefore, such behavior shall also not go unpunished. As the holy prophet Isaiah cries out against it: "Woe to those who justify the wicked for the sake of a bribe and who turn the just verdict of the righteous away from them." But if God commands a woe to be pronounced upon a man, that is surely said in earnest, not in jest. All paths must lead to this end, and through it, both land and people—indeed, even, at times a powerful kingdom—must come to ruin. For "it is on account of violence, injustice and greed through which justice is perverted that a kingdom passes from one people to another" (Sirach 10).

The Wisdom of Solomon has preached a sermon about this in chapter 6, where it says: "Unrighteousness makes all lands desolate, and a wicked life brings down the thrones of the powerful. So hear now, you kings! And you judges of the earth, mark and learn! Listen carefully, you who rule over many, who are exalted over the peoples, for authority has been given to you by the Lord, and power from the Most High, who will demand an accounting of your behavior and investigate your decrees. For you are officials of His kingdom. But you do not carry out your office rightly, nor do you uphold justice; and you do not do according to what the Lord has decreed. He will indeed come upon you dreadfully and quickly, and a stern judgment will indeed fall upon the rulers, for grace is given to the humble, but the powerful will be powerfully punished. For he who is Lord over all will fear no one, nor will He be afraid of their might." These harsh threats Solomon repeats in his sermon in chapter 3: "I saw under the sun: instead of judgment, wickedness was there; and instead of righteousness, wicked men were there. So I thought in my heart, God must judge the righteous and the wicked."

David, who occupied this estate of authority as a king, wrote a special Psalm [Psa. 82] as a warning for all authorities, to encourage them thereby to consider what a high office had been entrusted to them, how God Himself would be offended if they, in their office, acted lazily or casually, or if they showed partiality or dealt in any way contrary to justice and fairness, based on some personal preference they had. He says this: "God stands in the assembly of God and is Judge among the gods. How long will you judge according to injustice and show partiality to the wicked? Do justice to the poor and the fatherless and help the afflicted and the needy to get justice. Rescue the humble and the poor and deliver him from the violence of the wicked. But they refuse to hear and pay no attention. They always go about in darkness. Therefore all the foundations of the earth must fall. Surely I said, 'You are gods, and you are altogether children of the Most High. But you will die like men and come to ruin like a tyrant.' Arise, O God! For You are the inheritor over all nations."

Now, whatever has been said thus far concerning the high authorities, great rulers and governors, it must also be thoroughly understood that no less is demanded of councils, judges, officials, city and county councilmen, and, in general, of all those who are given authority by their masters to execute judgment and righteousness for others in their stead. For since the supreme rulers cannot be in all the places within their territory at once, they must have servants who help administer the government. Naturally, it is important to see to it that such offices are filled with pious, God-fearing individuals who love righteousness and sincerely oppose all unrighteousness.

Jethro, Moses' father-in-law, when he came to his son-in-law, the prophet Moses, and saw that the burden was too heavy for him to hear all the cases of the people and to render judgment for them all by himself, gave him some good advice: that he assign some men who could hear and judge the lesser cases and thus help to bear the burden of governing. He says: "Search among all the people for able men who fear God, who are truthful and hate covetousness. Set them over the people—over a thousand, over a hundred, over fifty, over ten—that they may judge the people at all times. But where a matter is too difficult, let them bring it to you, while they judge all the small matters. In this way it will be easier for you, if they bear the burden with you."

He enumerates three special virtues that should be found among the office-holders who would judge the people with, and alongside of, Moses. First, they should be God-fearing. This is the fountain of all goodness, a root of wisdom that makes the heart pious and that guards a man from evil. After that, truthful—those who sincerely love the truth in judgment and shun all sophistry that perverts justice. Third, hating covetousness. For covetousness is a root of all evil in one's entire life. Thus, where this vice reigns among judges, officials and councilmen, they cannot resist bribes and gifts, and accordingly justice is injured for the sake of a bribe, too much aid is given to the rich man while the poor is oppressed, and righteousness comes to utter ruin in the process.

Therefore, David also seeks pious, God-fearing, and able men whom he might have as assistants in managing such offices. In Psalm 101, he says: "My eyes watch the faithful in the land, that they may dwell with me, and that I may enjoy pious servants." When King Jehoshaphat ordained judges in all the cities of Judah, he addressed them and admonished them with these excellent words, which naturally apply to all counsel and should be written to any who come together to exercise judgment: "Observe carefully what you do, for you exercise judgment not for men, but for the Lord, and He is with you in the judgment. Therefore, let the fear of the Lord be with you, and guard yourselves and do it, for with the Lord our God there is neither injustice nor partiality nor the accepting of a bribe."

From this it is clear: whoever lets himself be swayed by bribe or favor or anything else to suppress the valid cases of the poor in court—such a judge has his own Judge standing right next to him, namely, the Lord God who sees, hears and knows such unjust abuse of power, and will, in His good time, bring it to light, judge it and punish it. For God will never despise the sighing of the oppressed. The poor commit their cause to Him, and He is the Helper of the fatherless, as is written in the Psalms. And again in Sirach 35: "The prayer of the humble pierces the clouds and does not rest until it reaches its goal; it does not cease until the Most High looks into it. And the Lord will judge and punish and will not relent nor be patient until He smashes the loins of the unmerciful and avenges Himself on such people and exterminates all those who do violence and overthrows the power of the unrighteous and gives to each one according to his works."

Therefore, even if it happens that someone else pronounces an unjust sentence or judgment, pious judges and councilmen should beware, and indeed, should not allow themselves to be seduced by another's example, lest they confirm such an unfair judgment with their voice and consent. For, in this matter, one is not dealing only with men, but with God, before whom one cannot simply give an account by going along with the crowd, for He has very clearly commanded in His law: "You shall not follow the crowd into evil, nor respond before the judgment that you departed from justice because of the crowd" (Exo. 23). And again in Isaiah 5: "Woe to those who tie themselves together with loose cords to commit iniquity, and with cart ropes to commit sin." Consequently, the surest path in such a case is for you to render your verdict and withdraw, for good cause, the unfair, perverted ruling of the other; or, if such a procedure would have no standing with them, then you should nevertheless let it be clearly understood that you do not concur with their verdict nor wish to participate in their sins. This is what Joseph of Arimathea did. He did not want to go along with the counsel of the other Jews against the Lord Jesus, and for this reason he has obtained an immortal commendation: to be praised by the Holy Spirit Himself as an honorable councilman and a good, pious man in the writings of the holy Evangelists.

In conclusion, then, it is fair that rulers should receive taxes, customs, and tribute from their subjects for the preservation of their estate, and also to benefit from their service in still other ways for the care and concern that they, as fathers of the fatherland, continually have for their subjects. Nevertheless, a Christian government that fears God must see to it that not too heavy a weight or burden is imposed on their subjects. On the contrary, they must promote the wellbeing of the poor subjects and seek to prosper them in all their ways. Otherwise, if one imposes too heavy a burden on one's subjects, their temporal livelihood is damaged so that, instead of being preserved by the protection of the government, they end up in poverty, become embittered toward their established authority (even though they shouldn't), and the godless among them, sighing under such a burden, curse God in heaven and His king on earth, as Isaiah says in chapter 8. But the pious and God-fearing among them, even though they do not curse, are unable to bear up under the burden of their sighing, and their sighing reaches heaven. Such abuse will also notably erode the sincere trust that should exist between government and subjects, and often leads the simple folk to fall away. This is demonstrated from the infamous example of King Rehoboam, who, when he threatened to make the former burdens (the ones the Israelites experienced under Solomon on account of the great building projects undertaken by him) even heavier, he caused so much trouble that in a single day ten tribes in Israel walked away from him.

The heathen have a saying: "It is the office of a good shepherd to sheer the sheep and to benefit from the wool, but not to skin them bare." How much more fitting it is for a Christian government to exercise due moderation in this matter so that they do not store up God's wrath, judgment and punishment for themselves, which He threatens through the prophet Micah with these earnest words: "Listen now, you chiefs of the house of Jacob, and you princes in the house of Israel! Is it not for you to know justice? But you hate the good and love the evil. You strip off their hide and the flesh from their bones, and you eat the flesh of My people. And after you have stripped off their hide, you also break their bones and carve them up as in a pot and as meat in a kettle. Therefore, when you cry out to the Lord, He will not listen to you, but will hide His face from you for the same amount of time as you have earned with your wicked ways."

Let this suffice concerning the vocation, estate, and office of a Christian ruler. May the almighty, eternal, merciful God, in whose hand all government on earth remains, deign to direct, guide and rule all the authorities with His Holy Spirit, that the saving knowledge of His beloved Son Jesus Christ may be embedded within their government, that the praise and honor of His divine Name may be extended, righteousness fostered, and wickedness hindered and punished, so that we may lead a peaceful and quiet life in all godliness and honor, and also, after this fleeting vale of tears, obtain through Christ eternal joy and blessedness. May God—Father, Son, and Holy Spirit—deign to help us to that end. Amen.

Fourth Sermon on the Table of Duties: Subjects in the Secular Realm

Romans 13

So, then, it is necessary that you be subject, not only because of punishment, but also for the sake of conscience. For this reason you must also pay taxes. For they are God's servants who should be attending to such protection. So, then, give to everyone what you owe them: taxes to whom taxes are due; customs to whom customs are due; fear to whom fear is due; honor to whom honor is due.

Dear Christians, in our explanation of the Table of Duties, we have been reflecting on the secular estate, and in the most recent sermon, we heard about the chief pillars of it, namely, the authorities and what they are to do or leave undone with regard to their office. Having considered this in detail, we now wish also to hear something about subjects: what they ought to render to their legitimate authorities on account of God's instruction and command.

We will treat distinctly each of the things we read above in the words of the apostle Paul, and we will consider them in order, one after the other.

SUBJECTS OWE THEIR AUTHORITIES HONOR

First of all, since the authorities are included in the Fourth Commandment (You shall honor father and mother) under the title of "fathers," and since we are instructed in the same commandment to honor fathers, it is clear that subjects are to render honor to the authorities no less than parents are to be honored by their children. Therefore, when St. Paul points out what is owed to the authorities, he mentions, among other things, honor. "Give honor to whom honor is due." They are to be honored, not only with external actions or with superficial reverence and homage, but this honor must be rooted in the heart in such a way that one recognizes them as a good and salutary ordinance of God, and thinks highly and honorably of them on account of the high office which they perform for God's sake, since for this very reason they are called "gods" and "children of the Most High." Sirach says in chapter 10: "Those who fear God hold their rulers in honor." St. Peter agrees with him. He says in chapter 2 of his First Epistle: "Fear God. Honor the king." From this it must follow that whoever does not hold his rulers in honor, in him there is no fear of God. For this reason, like some of the people of Israel who despised the newly elected King Saul, they will be reprimanded for it by the Holy Spirit and branded children of Belial, that is, children of the devil and rebels, as those who neither fear God nor honor their rulers.

But they commit an even graver sin who, contrary to this apostolic admonition of St. Paul, not only dishonor the legitimate authorities that have been placed over them, but curse them, revile them, profane and slander them, speak evil of them, and wish every unholy thing upon them—and this, contrary to God's earnest prohibition, thus stated in the Law of Moses in Exodus 22: "You shall not curse the gods (that is, the authorities), and the ruler in the midst of your people you shall not blaspheme." This is and is properly called "high treason," that is, the kind of sin in which pernicious, sacrilegious people do not hesitate (as Peter says in 2 Pet. 2) to show contempt for the authorities and to blaspheme the dignitaries, which, in the holy sight of God, is such a serious, intolerable sin that it is not only condemned in this life, but also punished with hellfire where men do not repent of it. That is what St. Peter means to say in the passage cited above concerning these blasphemers and mockers of the rulers: "They are like the brute beasts that are naturally born to be caught and destroyed. They blaspheme things they know nothing about. They will perish in their corrupt ways and receive for it the wages of unrighteousness."

Shimei, too, did not hesitate to blaspheme the royal majesty, to show contempt for his authority, and to curse the ruler of God's people. For when the godly King David was driven from the land by his son Absalom (2 Sam. 16) and came to Bahurim, Shimei came out and cursed and blasphemed with his godless jabber and said: "Get out! Get out, you bloodhound, you worthless man! The Lord has returned upon you all the blood of the house of Saul, in whose stead you became king. Now the Lord has given the kingdom into the hand of your son Absalom. And behold, now you are mired in your misfortune, for you are a bloodhound." Yet, although David spared him at that time out of extraordinary kindness and even swore an oath to him afterwards that he (during his own lifetime and rule) would not kill him, nevertheless the Lord God brought about his punishment in a remarkable way. For, after David's death, King Solomon ordered him not to leave Jerusalem and cross the Brook Kidron, or, if he did, he would surely die. Then, in order that his blasphemy and sacrilege against David might not remain unrequited, our Lord God brought it about that he was forced to chase after two of his slaves whom he pursued across the Brook Kidron so that he might be put to death according to the word of the king and thus receive his well-deserved reward. Indeed, this is the one thing God has imposed on all subjects through the mouth of the holy apostle Paul, that they should hold in all honor their governing officials who have been set up in the secular government. For "they are there in God's stead," whom God Himself has also dignified with His name. Now, if God has graced them with this honor, who are you that you should begrudge it to them, or that you would dare to rob them of it?

SUBJECTS OWE THEIR AUTHORITIES FEAR

Secondly, subjects also owe their authorities fear, according to the word and command of the apostle: "Give fear to whom fear is due." He does not mean here the kind of fear one must have of blood-thirsty, monstrous tyrants, some of whom live by this axiom: "They may hate, as long as they fear." In other words, "They may hate me, but it doesn't matter, as long as their hatred of me is accompanied by fear." For such a government seldom remains for long, being run by brute force so that the subjects are compelled to live in a constant state of fear, with their lives always in danger.

There is yet another kind of fear that is commended to godly, Christian subjects, different from the fear that is commended to the wicked who must be afraid of the authorities because of their sins and wickedness. Paul says of them: "Do you do evil? Then be afraid, for he does not bear the sword in vain."

But here, St. Paul means the kind of fear that is at the same time tempered and moderated with true love toward the authorities, so that one fears and is afraid of them as godly children are accustomed to fearing their parents, whom they love, and yet they are afraid to do anything against them. Now, let's say the authorities show themselves to be kind and gracious toward their subjects. Their subjects still shouldn't become too bold on account of such grace so that they think less of their rulers, or fear them less, or become overly casual about doing their duty, or impudently attempt to get away with things they shouldn't do. Rather, the fear and caution to which St. Paul urges us should remain in the heart: "Give fear to whom fear is due."

The holy man Job gives an outstanding example of this to his subjects as he says in his book, chapter 29: "Oh, that I were still as in former months, in the days when God cared for me, etc., when I would go out to the city gate and I would have my seat prepared for me in the square, when the young men saw me and hid, and the elders stood up in my presence, when the rulers stopped speaking and placed their hand over their mouth, when the voice of the princes was silenced and their tongue stuck to the roof of their mouth. For every ear that heard me praised me as blessed, and every eye that saw me extolled me." And shortly afterward in the same chapter he says: "They listened to me and remained silent and waited for my counsel. No one spoke again after my words, and my speech fell upon them. They waited upon me as upon the rain and shut up their mouth as after the evening rain. When I laughed with them, they did not become too bold because of it, and the light of my face did not make me smaller. When I wanted to come to their business, I was made to sit above, and I dwelt as a king among soldiers."

SUBJECTS OWE THEIR AUTHORITIES OBEDIENCE

Thirdly, Christians owe their leaders in the secular government submission and obedience toward all their commands and prohibitions, laws, and statutes that are in accord with, and not contrary to, God's Law and His holy Word. Paul especially drives home this requirement and also sets forth the basis and the reasons for admonishing Christians to such obedience. First, since this estate is ordained by God (as proven and explained in detail in the previous sermon), therefore whoever opposes it opposes God Himself as the Giver and Author of this good and salutary ordinance. Paul accordingly requires this obedience for conscience' sake. In doing so, he demonstrates that he who does not render this obedience can retain neither faith nor a good conscience. But a good and peaceful conscience is nobler and better than all the riches of the world. It is, as the Scripture teaches, a continual feast. How miserable it would be if a person had all the treasure on earth, but carried around in his chest a wicked, restless conscience that distressed and tormented him day and night without ceasing? If you do not wish to lose such a precious treasure as a good conscience, then be submissive and obedient to your authorities.

In addition to this, Paul says, one should be obedient to the established authorities also because of the punishment that awaits all the disobedient and recalcitrant. For those who oppose the authorities will receive judgment. This is already recorded in God's Word, and it will come upon them when they least expect it.

Disobedience especially cannot and may not go unpunished when the authorities are opposed with actual violence. That is, and is rightly called, insurrection and revolt, neither of which ever goes unpunished. Both the Holy Scriptures and daily experience teach us this and bear witness to it. Solomon writes in Proverbs 24: "My child, fear the Lord and the king; and do not associate with insurrectionists. For their downfall will occur suddenly. And who knows when misfortune will come upon him?" The Wisdom of Jesus Sirach agrees with Solomon in this matter, as he warns and says: "Do not commit insurrection in the city, and do not be attached to the mob, so that you do not bear double guilt, for neither will go unpunished." And in chapter 26, insurrection is numbered among the three terrible things that are an abomination to God and men.

There are also notable stories in the holy Bible that show, as an eternal remembrance, how horribly insurrectionists are always punished. Abimelech (Judges 9) drew to himself the unruly mob at Shechem, caused insurrection in Israel, received his reward for it by being dealt a deadly blow by a woman with a millstone, and was then run through by his armorbearer at his own request. Absalom (2 Sam. 18) rose up against the prince of God's people, his father King David, drove him out of the country, but in the end was hung on an oak tree, run through with a spear and smitten to death by Joab's armorbearer like a wild dog, and carried off to the devil without repentance and conversion (as one can easily surmise). And then, after the rebellion was quieted, Sheba, son of Bichri, incited a new mutiny and uprising to get Israel to fall away. Joab pursued him to the city of Abel, where the head of the rebels, Sheba, was thrown down to him over the city walls, and this insurgent was repaid for his dissipation, disloyalty, and disobedience. When the two captains Rechab and Baanah (2 Sam. 4) treacherously killed their own lord, the royal son of Saul, Ishbosheth, and took his head to King David, hoping to gain great favor with him for it, God's judgment came upon them suddenly. Their hands and feet were chopped off and they were hung up near the pool of Hebron as a dreadful example for all Israel.

When the ten tribes turned away from Rehoboam, their lord and king according to the flesh, in the arranged mutiny at

Shechem (1 Kings 12), such rebellious apostasy was terribly and severely punished. Since those who remained with the house of David under Rehoboam had the true worship and could serve God, the ten tribes were forced by their godless Jeroboam to serve idols so that, through idolatry, they were robbed of their poor souls' comfort and eternal salvation, and such idolatry increased among them more and more until the land couldn't bear them any longer (2 Kings 17). But according to God's judgment and threatening they had to be uprooted and carried off to a foreign land among their enemies and be miserably plagued with captivity and slavery.

King Ahasuerus' two eunuchs, Bigthan and Teresh, had plotted against him through disobedience, rebellion and treason, and had made an agreement to lay hands on the king. But this plot was discovered and revealed to the king by God's doing, and after the matter was investigated, they were hanged on a tree (Esther 2). So also, when Peter drew the sword against the servant of the high priest (Mat. 26), Christ warned him that he should cease in order that the judgment may not come upon him which is common to all rebels. For "whoever takes up the sword will die by the sword." In recent times we saw such a striking example of this in the peasants' revolt that it will never be forgotten until the end of time, namely, how the peasants, instigated and persuaded by a few Anabaptist preachers, took up arms and revolted against their rulers, princes, counts, etc. But the terrible judgment of God caught up with them, so that many thousands died here and there in various lands, and the majority of them perished, body and soul, temporally and eternally.

In summary, it proven by all these examples that he who opposes the authority will receive judgment. But whoever wishes to escape and be freed from this judgment must follow the teaching of St. Paul, to be obedient and subject. For this he will be praised, and he will be able to retain a good conscience.

This commandment concerning obedience on the part of the subjects is not so often repeated in the New Testament for no reason. For the Holy Spirit knows best of all how much depends on this. In his Epistle to Titus, chapter 3, the apostle writes: "Remind them to be subject and obedient to the rulers and authorities." And St. Peter, in his First Epistle, chapter 2, says: "Be subject to every ordinance of men for the Lord's sake, whether to the king as the highest ruler, or to the officials as those sent by him to bring wrath against the evildoers and praise to the godly. For it is God's will that you should silence the ignorance of foolish men by doing good."

But here we must take note how far this obedience extends. For if the secular authority would command something that goes against God, His Word, justice and equity, then one is not bound to render them any obedience in such wicked matters. In such a case, the words of St. Peter apply: "One must rather be obedient to God than to men" (Acts 5). Indeed, one should be willing to suffer all things rather than do anything against God and his own conscience in order to please his earthly rulers.

Pharaoh, king of Egypt, commanded the Hebrew midwives (Exo. 1) to kill all the Israelite baby boys as soon as they were born into the world. But the midwives feared God (says Moses) and did not do what the king in Egypt commanded, but allowed the children to live. God also rewarded them richly for this and built up their houses, that is, He granted good fortune, blessing and prosperity to their household affairs. King Saul's officials also acted justly and worthily in this manner (1 Sam. 22) when they did not follow the royal decree that they should put innocent men—the 85 priests of the Lord—to death. The officials would have nothing to do with this decree, and they behaved far better than the wicked Edomite Doeg, who executed and carried out this evil command of the king.

But especially when it comes to religion, true and genuine faith, and pure and unadulterated worship, subjects neither can nor should repudiate or abandon these things in order to please their rulers. For that would mean abandoning the Lord God Himself and repudiating the Word of the Most High. Therefore Christ has set a goal and a boundary for how far and how broadly we are bound to obey secular authority, saying: "Give to Caesar what is Caesar's, and to God what is God's" (Mat. 22). In all things that are not opposed to God, one should be obedient to the authorities. But God Himself makes the exception that no one should sin in order to please man, especially if it means abandoning the genuine faith for the service of men or accepting idolatry or false teaching.

For this reason also the three companions of the prophet Daniel were not to be blamed for refusing to worship the idolatrous image that King Nebuchadnezzar had set up (Dan. 3), even though the king had commanded everyone to do it. Instead, they preferred to be thrown into the fiery furnace, explaining themselves before the king with these words: "Behold, our God, whom we serve, can surely deliver us from the burning furnace and also rescue us from your hand. And if He is unwilling to do so, you should still know that we will not serve your gods nor worship the golden image that you have set up." Something similar happened when King Darius, at the instigation of some of his counselors, issued a decree (Dan. 6) that, for thirty days, anyone who prayed for anything from a god or from any man except for the king should be thrown into the lions' den. The holy prophet Daniel knew better than to obey this wicked decree and command of the king. On the contrary, he openly directed his prayer to his Lord and God with the window to his house wide open, and he preferred to be thrown into the lions' den rather than to obey this command against God and His holy worship. God also came to his aid miraculously in the lions' den, just as He had graciously helped Daniel's friends in the fiery furnace in Babylon.

Therefore, if something is commanded that cannot be obeyed with a good conscience, then God-fearing Christians should focus on God and obey Him rather than men in such a matter. Even if they forfeit the favor of men in the process, they nevertheless retain God's favor and grace, and He is more than able to make up for it. On the other hand, no matter how high and mighty they may be, men cannot make up for it if someone sins in order to please them and is carried off to the devil for it. At the same time, it is not permissible under any circumstances for subjects to oppose the authorities with public violence. True, they should not be obedient to them in wicked matters. Nevertheless, they also should not resort to violence, but should rather suffer for it, as the aforementioned examples of Daniel and his companions demonstrate.

SUBJECTS OWE THEIR RULERS TAXES, CUSTOMS, ETC.

Furthermore and fourthly the apostle Paul wants Christians to be admonished to give their rulers tribute, customs, taxes and such things. "This is also why you must pay taxes," he says, "for they are God's servants who attend to such protection." Likewise: "So, then, give to everyone what you owe them: taxes to whom taxes are due; customs to whom customs are due."

Indeed, pious Christians should be found doing this willingly, first, on account of God's commandment, since He expressly commands it through the mouth of the holy apostle Paul. Christ also confirmed it with His clear command when the Jews asked Him whether they should pay the temple tax to Caesar or not (Mat. 22). When, at His request, they showed Him the coin for paying the tax on which was imprinted the image and inscription of the high authority, He said: "Give to Caesar what is Caesar's, and to God what is God's." He reinforced this with His own example by giving the temple tax to those who came from the high authority requiring it (Mat. 17). God also ordained it in this way among His own people, that they should give the tithe and other such things to the king, as Samuel described for the people of Israel the right of the king (1 Sam. 8). In the same account it was pointed out to them that the king would take the tithe from their harvest and from their vineyard, as well as from their herds, in order that he might pay his officials and servants.

Beyond that, it is indeed fair to be helpful to the authorities with taxes, duties, tribute and so on, so that through this help in the form of taxes and allowances, everything is accomplished and carried out that is necessary for the preservation, not only of their estate, but also of the common necessities, good civil affairs and government, and of a necessary stockpile in the event of a future war against the enemy of the fatherland.

Fairness also demands this, since the authorities bear the burden and care for land and people, and, as Paul says, they, "must attend to this protection," so that, indeed, the subjects show themselves grateful toward them in countless ways, and thus also with taxes, customs, duties, and more.

For, to be sure, they can never repay Christian rulers with any amount of gold for all the good that they experience from them, namely, each one can sit down in good rest and noble peace under his own vine and fig tree, under the shade of the authorities (as the Scriptures describe this benefit). Otherwise, if there were no authority, no one could keep himself safe and free in the presence of another—nor his possessions, nor that which God provides for his sustenance. But, on account of the profuse wantonness of evil knaves, he would have such a savage existence that whoever was stronger than his neighbor would immediately smother him and take from him all that God had given him.

Next to God, it is the authorities that we have to thank for the fact that everyone can live in tranquility on his own property. They suppress wantonness with the sword so that the common peace remains undisturbed and each one's property remains untouched. Whoever considers this from a Christian perspective must conclude in his heart that it is truly fair and just that the rulers should also benefit from some of our possessions and goods, since they are sufficiently defended against enemies and other evil men through the protection and shelter of the authorities.

But if it should happen that a ruler weren't satisfied with a fair amount and demanded more from his subjects than they could afford, and if the pleas and petitions of the subjects to remove such a burden went unheeded by the authorities, even so God does not permit anyone to rise up against the rulers with violence because of it, or to give the required tribute begrudgingly. For although God takes no pleasure in such a burden and will not allow it to go unnoticed, as explained in the previous sermon, and although the ruler commits a grave sin in imposing it in that he expects too much of the poor subjects entrusted to his care, nevertheless the subjects are not committing a sin if they give the required tribute. On the contrary, they are duty-bound in this matter to bear the burden, since God demands in His holy divine Word that one should also be obedient to spiteful rulers.

Indeed, they ought to give thanks to God that He has up till now graciously preserved them from the horrible, miserable, deplorable tribute that the Christians who live under the Turkish emperor must render. They are forced to have their own dear children follow him. He has them brought up from childhood onward in the blasphemous, damned Mohammedan unbelief, and when they are grown up, they are then used in battle against the holy Christendom, and in this way they are led away from their Lord and Redeemer Jesus Christ and placed into the utmost danger of forfeiting their souls' salvation—indeed, they are stuck in the devil's throat. Oh, how many thousands of times more bearable is every temporal tax and tribute that one pays so that, living under the protection of Christian authorities, he may have the precious, valuable treasure of the saving knowledge of Jesus Christ from the preached Word, and may bring up his dear children therein, as in a heavenly pasture.

SUBJECTS OWE THEIR RULERS KINDNESS, LOVE, AND LOYALTY

Therefore, in the fifth place they owe their rulers kindness, love, and loyalty, so that in every way, as much as possible, they should alert them of trouble and, if their rulers are in danger, faithfully run to their aid, even risking life and limb for their sake if necessary. Many fine examples of such loyalty and love can be found in the history of King David. We see it, for instance, in Ittai the Gittite (2 Sam. 15), who, when he was about to follow the king into exile and the king admonished him to turn around, answered: "As surely as the Lord lives, wherever my lord the king shall be, should it result in death or in life, there shall your servant be also." Similar loyalty was demonstrated by Hushai (2 Sam. 17), who, on account of his great loyalty and love toward David, is called David's friend by the Holy Spirit. He also thwarted the counsel of wicked Ahithophel and sent a message to the king warning him of the danger. And when David wanted to go out to join the battle (2 Sam. 18), his soldiers, as loyal subjects, wouldn't let him fall into this danger, but answered him: "You must not go out, for even if we flee or half of us die, they will not care about us. For you are worth ten thousand of us." There is yet another example, when he was in jeopardy of life and limb in a war with the Philistines (2 Sam. 21) on account of a giant uncircumcised Philistine named Ishbi who came far too close to him, such that David was narrowly rescued by Abishai, who struck the Philistine dead and came to the aid of the king. His people then swore to the king and said: "You must no longer go out with us into battle, that the light in Israel may not be extinguished." All of these are examples of faithful subjects whom the Spirit of God Himself has mentioned with special honor. And the loyalty of the godly Jew Mordechai is praised no less for warning King Xerxes about the two officials who plotted against his life (Esther 2). This is how all Christian, godly subjects are minded toward their authorities and should be loyal and true to them, as they are commanded and sworn to do.

SUBJECTS ARE OBLIGED TO PRAY FOR THE AUTHORITIES

In the sixth and final place, godly subjects are obliged on account of God's commandment to offer general prayer and intercession for their rulers. For Paul commanded this when he wrote to his disciple Timothy in 1 Timothy 2: "I hereby admonish, first of all, that prayers, petitions, intercession and thanksgiving be offered for all men—for kings and for all authorities, so that we may lead a peaceful and quiet life in all godliness and honor." St. Paul earnestly presses Timothy that he shouldn't forget, but rather make it the first priority in the church that prayers should be diligently offered for the secular authorities. For if the authorities are believers and sympathetic to the Christian religion, then one should pray that God would preserve them in the knowledge of Him and in all goodness, so that the subjects, too, might enjoy the pure worship of God. Or, if the authorities are unbelievers or idolaters, then one has reason to pray, on the other hand, that God would enlighten them, and that they would reign in such a way that they may begin to make room for the doctrine of the holy Gospel and open the gates of their rule to the King of glory (Psa. 24).

Even if they persecute the Gospel, the general prayer still must not be denied them, for Paul calls on Christians to pray for all the authorities (which, at that time, were almost entirely heathen and opposed to the Gospel). And Jeremiah writes a letter to the captive Jewish people in Babylon (Jer. 29) in which he, among other things, also directs them to seek the good of the state to which they have been taken, and to pray to the Lord for it. Such a prayer serves the interest of the subjects themselves. For God, who holds the heart of the authorities in His almighty hand (Pro. 21), can and will, in gracious consideration of such an intercession made by believers, influence and steer the rulers to good and turn them away from much evil. He has also promised to hear the prayer of every single Christian, to listen intently when a group of them come together in prayer, as it is written: "Where two of you unite on earth on what it is you wish to ask for, it shall be done for you by My Father in heaven" (Mat. 18).

May God the Father of our Lord Jesus Christ, together with the Holy Spirit, graciously give and grant us that, in the aforementioned ways, we may prove to be Christian subjects toward the authorities that have been placed over us: to honor and fear them, to render them due submission and obedience, to give them willingly what we owe them, to be loyal and kind to them from the heart, and to commend them to the Lord God unceasingly with believing prayer, that we may be heard both for their wellbeing and for ours. To this one true God be glory, honor and praise forever and ever. Amen.

Fifth Sermon:
Husbands and Wives

To Husbands:
Husbands, love your wives, just as Christ loved the Church and gave Himself for her in order that He might sanctify her, having purified her by the water-washing in the Word, that He might present her to Himself as a Church that is glorious, that has neither blemish nor wrinkle or anything of the kind, but that she may be holy and blameless. In this way also, husbands should love their wives as their own bodies. He who loves his wife loves himself. For no one ever hated his own flesh, but nourishes and cares for it, just as also the Lord does with the Church.

To Wives:
Wives, be submissive to your husbands as to the Lord. For the husband is the head of the wife, just as Christ is the Head of the Church, and He is the Savior of His body. But now, as the Church is submissive to Christ, so also wives should be to their husbands in all things.

Beloved in the Lord Christ, now that, in the explanation of our Christian Table of Duties, we have spoken and heard from God's Word about two chief estates, the spiritual and the secular, there remains still the third estate, which is and is called the domestic estate. It covers the entire realm of the home, including husband and wife, parents and children, masters and menservants, mistresses and maidservants. Now, since the other two estates—the spiritual and secular realms—are derived from this domestic estate, and since practically all men are involved with it, because there is no one who is neither husband nor wife, master nor manservant, mistress nor maidservant, necessity requires that also in this estate Christians be faithfully reminded from God's Word of their office and vocation.

So, then, since man and woman living in the estate of matrimony are the foremost heads and pillars in the domestic estate, we must have a clear explanation of these things: (1) what the holy estate of matrimony entails; (2) how the husband should regard and behave toward his wife; and (3) how the wife should regard and behave toward her husband.

PART 1

As a wretched enemy of every good ordinance of God, Satan has attacked that which pertains to the estate of matrimony no less than he has also attacked the estate of secular authority by means of restless spirits and false teachers, and has undertaken to brand it as a sinful estate. For not only did he incite certain heretics long ago, like the Encratitics who degraded marriage as far as possible, but he has also forcefully promoted the same thing in Christendom through the wretched Antichrist, the Roman pope. It is widely known, both from the books of the papists and from their public deeds, how they have depicted marriage to the people as something carnal. They have insinuated that man cannot serve God in this estate with a clear conscience. Thus, in good antichristian fashion, they have interpreted Paul's saying, "Those who live in the flesh cannot please God," with respect to the estate of matrimony. Indeed, with such ungodly false teaching they have prevailed to such a degree that even great lords and ladies of the princes and counts, as well as married men and women among the nobility, have abandoned the estate of marriage. The husband hands himself over to a monastery, the wife to a nunnery, all for the sake of doing penance with the supposed holiness of monasticism for the sins they committed in the married estate. As a result, the antichristian papistic prohibition is issued that this estate should be completely forbidden to the whole spiritual order. From this marriage-free life, innumerable and horrible sins have arisen, especially the Sodomite abomination. These will be revealed in due time on the Last Day, and it will not be good when it becomes thoroughly known how the supposedly spiritual men have behaved in the whole world under the guise and label of virginity.

But if we listen to the Holy Spirit's own judgment concerning the married estate, we discover something much different than what the papists suggest. For He thoroughly extols it in the Holy prophetic and apostolic Scriptures and lauds and praises it as a good and irreproachable ordinance. He points out that God Himself instituted and ordained marriage (Genesis 1). As it is written: "God created man in His own image. Yes, in the image of God He made him; He made them a man and a woman. And God blessed them and said to them: 'Be fruitful and multiply, and fill the earth, and make it subject to you.'" And again: "The Lord God said: 'It is not good for the man to be alone. I will make him a helper who is comparable to him" (Gen. 2). But whatever God Himself makes, does, and ordains certainly must not be rebuked by men as sinful, but must be recognized as praiseworthy and good.

In addition, God has not only ordained that the human race should be propagated, multiplied, and preserved through the married companionship of man and woman, but it is also God's will and command that whoever does not have the special gift to live a chaste and decent life outside of marriage should pursue this estate of marriage in a legitimate way. "To avoid harlotry," says St. Paul, "let each man have his own wife, and each woman her own husband." And "the one who marries does not commit a sin, but does well," as Paul writes to his Corinthians.

But since the apostle says in the same place, "It is good for the man not to touch a woman," the papists have established their practice of supposed celibacy or the unmarried life and want to ascribe to it special power and merit before the Lord God. Nevertheless, it is obvious that it never entered St. Paul's mind either to diminish the estate of marriage with these words or to place virginity ahead of marriage, as if it were somehow more meritorious. For Christ alone has merited everything for us. We merit nothing with our deeds except hell, if God wished to reckon with us, whether we are in the married estate or outside of it. There is likewise also no partiality in Christ Jesus, whether a person is called master or servant, Jew or Greek, man or woman, married or virgin. But with the words previously cited from the Apostle Paul, he was considering the situation in the present time, as he expressly explains, saying: "So, then, I think that this (namely, that a man not touch a woman) is good, on account of the present need." For since at that time the authorities in Corinth were heathens and were constantly trying to lay hold of the Christians, they might be chased away from their property and goods into poverty, in which case it was much more difficult for married folk to be driven away with their children than for those who had no such dependents, but had instead an unfettered existence. It was only and alone the reality of the present need at that time that the apostle had in view, as he explains with clear words, and it was only for this reason that he wrote that, given the circumstances, it was good for a man not to touch a woman.

Furthermore, the married estate does not hinder a man in any way concerning his salvation. On the contrary, St. Paul expressly writes concerning women (1 Tim. 2) that "the woman will be saved through bearing children," that is, she will not at all be hindered concerning her salvation through bearing children and other marital works, "but only if she remains in faith and love and holiness, with propriety," even as the dear, holy patriarchs and matriarchs, as well as many prophets lived in the married estate, bore children, and were no less acceptable to God in heaven because of it. Indeed, even the Old Testament priests lived in the married estate, such that God Himself prescribes for them what kind of wives they should take, as we see in the third book of Moses, chapter 21. Therefore, it is God and His holy ordinance that the papists were disparaging when, in former times, they held the married estate to be sinful, and even to the present day they do not count it worthy enough for spiritual people like them to live in it, as if they might contaminate their antichristian reputation through it. The highly enlightened apostle Paul rightly labels this a demonic doctrine when, rich in the Spirit, he prophesies and speaks of the kingdom of the Antichrist and his deceptive doctrine. "But the Spirit says with certainty that in the last days, some will turn away from the faith and give heed to deceiving spirits and doctrines of demons, through those who are liars in hypocrisy and have a hot branding iron in their conscience, and forbid to marry, and command to abstain from the food that God has created."

Here Paul is not only prophesying about the Encratitic heretics—the papists would gladly whitewash themselves, casting this prophecy away from themselves and onto the Encratitics. But he is preaching chiefly about those who, in the last times (as his words clearly say), would forbid marriage and food, which is fulfilled in the papacy, as opposed to the Encratitics, who came soon after the apostle and against whom the ancient teacher Irenaeus wrote. The apostle is also not speaking about a small sect, as were the Encratitics who had no significant following and quickly fizzled out. No, he has in mind a special, notable deception that would arise under the reign of Antichrist. He most surely did not say, "If the Encratitics forbid marriage, it should be considered heresy. But if the pope forbids it, it should be considered a sacred act." No, he simply states universally that if anyone forbids marriage to people whom God has made fit for it, whether in the spiritual or secular realm, the Holy Spirit, through the mouth of the apostle Paul, has branded him a teacher of the devil, no matter who he may be or what title he may have. Let the issue be settled with this.

For God surely wants marriage to remain unforbidden also to spiritual persons, that is, to bishops, teachers and preachers, as it is written in 1 Timothy 3, a bishop must be the husband of one wife. He must have well-disciplined children. He must rule his own house well, or else, if he does not rule his own house well, how, then, will he be able to care for the Church of God? It is and remains a good estate, of which neither the Old Testament priests nor the New Testament bishops or teachers had anything to be ashamed. For if marriage were an impure estate, the Son of God would never have used it in Holy Scripture to depict the great mystery of the spiritual bond, faithfulness and love between Him and His dear Bride, the Christian Church, much less would He have graced the wedding at Cana with His most holy presence or honored it with His first miracle. But given that He does, He shows and clearly demonstrates that He recognizes marriage as a divine ordinance that should be highly honored by everyone, as the Epistle to the Hebrews also teaches in chapter 13.

PART 2

Now that we have set forth from God's Word how we are to view and esteem the estate of marriage, we will, in the name of God, address the specific duties of both husband and wife.

Indeed, this is what St. Paul prescribes to husbands in the previously read words of our lesson: **Husbands, love your wives, just as Christ loved the Church and gave Himself for her, etc.**

With the single word "love," he has encompassed all that a Christian husband is to perform for his wife. He does not present this admonition without context, but illustrates it with excellent patterns and examples. With patterns, in that he says they should love their wives "as their own bodies. For whoever loves his wife loves himself, since no one ever hated his own flesh." With these words, he reminds husbands of the close relationship that husband and wife have as one flesh and one body with one another, even as Adam recognized when his dear Eve was brought to him and, full of the Holy Spirit, he burst forth with these words: "This is now bone of my bones and flesh of my flesh. She shall be called 'woman,' for she was taken out of the man. For this reason a man will leave his father and mother and cleave to his wife, and the two shall become one flesh" (Genesis 2). For since the highest form of relationship exists between spouses in that they are reckoned as one flesh and one body, the highest form of love should certainly also exist between them, such that a man also leaves his own parents, cleaves to his wife in love, faithfulness, and married companionship, and abandons her neither in love nor in sorrow.

Therefore they are not men at all who hate their wives, that is, who hate their own flesh and blood, are cruel and mean to them, and begrudge them a kind word. This properly comes from the instigation of the wretched devil, who foments such hatred in the hearts of many stubborn, savage, godless husbands in order to ruin the good institution of God among them.

In connection with this, St. Paul also introduces the famous, excellent example of the inexpressible love of Christ for His dear, precious Christian Church in order to move husbands to imitate it by thinking of the wives given to them by God with true and genuine love, and by treating them accordingly. For surely the faithfulness and love with which Christ embraces His Church are not small nor cold nor lukewarm, but have been proven mightily with incontrovertible works and shown to be utterly fervent, sincere and genuine, since He even gave His life for her and has purchased and won her with His holy, precious blood. Thus the apostle concludes that husbands, too, should truly love their wives from the bottom of their hearts, as Adam loved his Eve, as Abraham loved Sarah, as Isaac loved Rebecca. Their love for their wives has been exalted by the Holy Spirit.

Nevertheless, this love has its proper measure and limit, that one should not love his wife in such a way that it causes him to forget love toward God and His Word, nor to sin in order to please her. There are plenty of husbands who are unable to refuse their wives anything, no matter how unjust it may be. Adam would have done far better if he had refused his Eve's offer and had not eaten from the forbidden fruit. Solomon, too, would have acted more wisely if he had not permitted idolatry to be established in Israel in order to please his foreign wives. And Ahab would have been much slower to permit sin if he had not allowed himself to be talked into so many unseemly things due to his perverse love for his Jezebel.

Therefore, love for one's wife must not be contrary to, but subordinate to love for God. Such a true, proper love is presented by God in the Scriptures and commended to husbands.

Men should further be moved to this noble love by the fact that, just as through it, all sorts of Christian virtues are sown, so also, where it is suppressed through the bitterness of one's heart, then all Christian practices, especially prayer, utterly fall to pieces.

For this reason, Paul especially writes concerning husbands that they should lift up clean hands in prayer, without anger and without doubting. With these words, he means to teach that, if they do not love their wives but are angry, bitter, and harsh with them, then they cannot pray; their prayer is in vain and without any fruit, just as if it flowed from an unchristian heart, being made with unclean hands. That which is written in the prophet Isaiah, chapter 1, also pertains to this: "Even though you spread out your hands, I will hide My eyes from you. And even if you pray much, I will not hear you, for your hands are full of blood."

He who prays and then again curses (as many men do, unfortunately)—how shall the Lord pay attention to him?, says Sirach in chapter 35.

Therefore, when St. Peter in like measure wants to admonish husbands to love their spouses, he mentions this central reason alongside it, "that your prayer may not be hindered." For where there is prayer, there is all grace and blessing, which are obtained from God through the believing prayer.

This is also why the sacrifices of the priests at the time of the prophet Malachi were unacceptable, because sin reigned among them at that time in that they made life miserable for their wives and were very harsh and merciless toward them, as the Lord says in Malachi 2: "Furthermore, you also do this: you bring tears and weeping and sighing before the altar of the Lord, so that I may no longer regard the offering nor receive anything from your hands as acceptable. And so you say: Why? This is why, because the Lord is witness between you and the wife of your youth whom you despise, although she is your companion and a wife of your covenant." Christian husbands should certainly take all these things to heart and love their wives according to the command of the Holy Spirit. Such genuine, heartfelt love also brings with it extraordinary patience, so that, although the wife has some human weakness or frailty, her husband, nevertheless, regards her kindly for it, or, indeed, seeks to remove it from her in as friendly a way as possible and orders all things to the end that the peace of the house, trust, love, and unity may not be disturbed.

And if the two should have an argument (which is unavoidable, with so many different issues that arise in a marriage), they must diligently see to it that they are reconciled quickly and without delay, that the sun is not allowed to set upon their anger, so that a persistent hatred and grudge may not grow out of it and cause eternal, irreversible harm.

Besides, what good can ever come from impatience, bitterness, quarrels, and constant strife? What else can result when there is constant arguing and fighting but that they lose God's grace and blessing—yes, even the Holy Spirit? They make this fleeting life bitter. They have to suffer through this life only to suffer even more in the next, and they are unable to know gratitude, but only adversity.

Experience shows that, once the wretched devil is given such an opportunity to set foot in the home, it is very hard to drive him out again. He keeps fueling the fire, so that disunity is nurtured, the hearts of the spouses grow further and further apart, and the rift between them becomes so great and so harmful that it not only leads to adultery in many cases, but even murder and other calamities sometimes result from such disunity. St. Peter has given husbands a stern warning in this regard: "Husbands," he says, "dwell with your wives with understanding, and give to the wife her honor, as to the weakest vessel, as those who are also coheirs of the grace of life."

Since this also pertains to the chief point in the lesson that Paul is presenting to husbands, that they love their wives, they must likewise also be taught not to direct this love toward other women, but to keep their hearts focused on those alone whom God has given and granted to them, clinging to them alone with marital faithfulness, as the heavenly wisdom teaches in Proverbs 5, saying: "Rejoice in the wife of your youth. She is lovely as a doe and pleasant as a deer. Let her love satisfy you at all times, and delight always in her love. My child, why should you delight in the stranger and cuddle with another? For the ways of every man are before the Lord, and He ponders all their paths. The iniquity of the wicked will ensnare him, and he will be bound with the cord of his sin."

God, in His Word, has forbidden this sin that so strongly opposes marital love and faithfulness and has branded it a damning sin by which the eternal salvation of souls is forfeit. For "no adulterer will have a share in the kingdom of God" (Galatians 5). And "God will judge the adulterer and fornicator" (Heb. 13). Thus, if they will not turn back from all this, they surely have the eternal punishment, agony, and torment of hell to expect. Nor will they escape temporal punishment in this life. As Jesus Sirach has taught in this proverb: "A man who commits adultery," he says, "and thinks to himself, 'Who sees me? No one sees me. Whom shall I fear? The Most High pays no attention to my sin,' fears only the eyes of men and does not consider that the eyes of the Lord are far brighter than the sun, and see all that men do, and peer even into secret corners. Such a man will be punished publicly in the city and will be caught when he least expects it." The story of King David demonstrates how horribly God punished him with temporal punishments on account of his adultery. And it is revealed in Holy Scripture that God condemned the ancient world with the Flood on account of such sins. He wiped out Sodom and Gomorrah with fire and brimstone from heaven, and whole countries and kingdoms were brought to ruin because of it. Indeed, the whole duty of a husband is contained in this one word "love," and it extends into all the other duties that flow from it.

PART 3

But what is the corresponding duty of Christian, reputable, godly wives? St. Paul has explained it to them in this way: "Let wives be submissive to their husbands as to the Lord, etc." Thus submission and obedience are required of them. But in order that they may not be given to complaining about this, the dear Apostle has, at the same time, chosen to accompany this command with his certain, lovely and stirring reasons for it. First he says: "They should be submissive to their husbands as to the Lord." He gives them to understand that, if they were to refuse to obey, they would be opposing God Himself as the One who has so ordained it that the wife should be subject to the husband. For this is what God imposed on the woman after the first fall: "Your will shall be subject to your husband, and he shall be your master" (Genesis 3).

We find this divine will and commandment often renewed and repeated in the Scriptures. In 1 Corinthians 11, St. Paul ordains how man and woman are to behave in the congregation and public assembly with outward behavior, and teaches that the man indeed should pray with uncovered head, while the woman should pray with her head covered, in order to show that the woman is subject to the man. As an outward sign of this, her head should be covered, for the man did not come from the woman, but the woman from the man, and the man was not created for the sake of the woman, but the woman for the sake of the man. Indeed, Paul writes to his disciple Titus that he should teach the young women to be submissive to their husbands. Therefore, he will not permit them to teach in the public congregation, nor to rule over the men (1 Timothy 2). St. Paul explained this admonition to the women with the beautiful example of the Church (or "congregation"), which is also submissive to her heavenly Bridegroom, Christ Jesus, hears His voice and follows Him.

Since, then, God the Lord has revealed this as His command, will, and intention, pious, God-fearing women should not view this ordinance of God as being opposed to them. They should know that, if they render this obedience, they are thereby rendering obedience to the Lord Himself and to His holy ordinance. And if, in all reasonable, decent, godly matters, they willingly view this humility in a positive light and are obedient to their husbands in quietness and gentleness with the intention of honoring God and His commandment, then they obtain glory thereby in the presence of God, the elect angels, and pious men who love honor.

And isn't this the smallest part of the adornment that St. Peter requires of women, namely, if they are submissive to their husbands? As a model and example, he directs their attention to the holy women who placed their hope in God and were submissive to their husbands. He especially makes mention of the blessed matriarch Sarah, who was obedient to Abraham and called him "master." All Christian women are her daughters, if they do good and show themselves to follow in her praiseworthy footsteps. Such women are referred to in the Scriptures as reasonable women, a noble gift, a crown to their husbands, more to be preferred than precious pearls and all gold, among the nine things that the wise husband will praise with his mouth. And as the sun is an ornament in the heavens above, so is such a virtuous wife an ornament in her house.

On the other hand, those women who turn their eyes away from this commandment and ordinance of God, who are not submissive to their husbands and do not prove obedient but oppose them with a stubborn and angry demeanor, bitterness, and obstinacy—they wear a mark of shame around their necks. As for what God Himself thinks of them, they can read about it in the 25th chapter of the book of the Wisdom of Sirach, where it is written about them: "I would rather dwell with lions and dragons than with an evil woman. When she becomes evil and angry, she changes her expression and becomes as dreadful as sackcloth. Her husband must be ashamed of her. And if someone reproaches him for it, it pains his heart." And shortly thereafter it is written: "An evil wife brings sorrow to the soul, sadness to the countenance, and suffering to the heart. A woman in whom a husband finds no friend causes him disappointment at every turn."

Therefore, if you are a wife and the thought ever occurs to you that you should not give any preference to your husband, since, after all, you come from a family that is just as noble as his, you are just as rich as he is, just as smart and intelligent as he is, then quickly reconsider: From whom might such a thought proceed? Your conscience will just as quickly tell you, it comes not from the good and Holy Spirit (for He would have wives obey their husbands), but from the wretched devil who would gladly overturn God's ordinance so that the woman is not obedient to her husband, but rebellious. But by listening to the devil, such women are considered evil by all God-fearing Christians. And God punishes such perverse arrogance, since they refuse to be obedient under their husbands in humility, so that they are finally struck down and brought to ridicule and ruin.

When Queen Vashti was disobedient to the order of her husband, King Ahasuerus, and refused to come at his bidding, she was stripped by public decree of all her royal dignity and glory so that she should no longer be queen or the wife of King Ahasuerus. She serves as a warning to all women, that they may learn from her to honor their husbands at all times, both in great and small matters, as it is written in the first chapter of the Book of Esther. She was replaced by the poor, humble maiden Esther, who, after she was exalted to the position of queen, behaved with due submission toward her master and husband and thus experienced great fortune and success, having found satisfaction in her submission.

As for the other things that pertain to the obedience of a noble woman, that will be discussed more fully on another occasion. But the summary of that discussion is that she should be temperate in words and actions, that she be self-controlled, chaste, busy at home, and kind; that she love her children and conduct herself with true fear of God and reverence; that she be adorned with modesty and discipline, as is proper for women who demonstrate godliness through good works. Likewise, that she attend to the management of the home and work gladly with her hands, as the domestic affairs of a virtuous woman are masterfully described and enumerated one by one in the Proverbs of Solomon (Pro. 31). Such a married woman "pursues the noble life," says Solomon again in Proverbs 6[4]. She makes a fine, peaceful life for her husband. Her husband's heart should rely on her, and he will never lack provisions. She brings him love his whole life through and never sorrow (Pro. 31, Sirach 26). She is like a merchant vessel that brings provisions from afar. She will be praised by the fruits of her hands, and her works will herald her at the gates. She obtains an immortal name and is praised for generations to come.

Where husband and wife live together with one another in this manner, as we have now thoroughly explained—in the fear of God, in true love, peace, quietness, and unity—what gift among all temporal gifts could be nobler or better? This is one of the three beautiful things that please both God and men (Sirach 25). When man and wife get along well with one another, there God will be, together with His dear angels. There He will grant blessings, and even the many burdens of the married life will be much easier to bear. They are able to lead a quiet life, and they will finally be preserved by Christ the Lord in the true faith in Him for eternal salvation. May God—Father, Son, and Holy Spirit—deign to help us all to that end. Amen.

---

4 According to Luther's translation of Pro. 6:26.

Sixth Sermon:
Parents, Fathers and Mothers

Ephesians 6[5]

Fathers, do not provoke your children to anger, that they may not become discouraged. But bring them up in the training and admonition of the Lord.

We have before us in the explanation of the Table of Duties the domestic estate; that is, the government of the home. We were just reminded in the previous sermon about the first order of this estate, namely, that of husband and wife as the chief persons in it, how the husband ought to carry out his duty toward his wife, and the wife toward her husband. But God instituted this marital and domestic estate for the purpose of raising children, and through this ordinance the human race is preserved and increased. In this way, a Church is also gathered to God and to our Lord Jesus Christ, so that He may be known here on earth and praised there in eternity. Therefore, the natural order here requires that we speak about parents and children and how they are to treat one another.

We wish on this occasion to say something about the office of the parents—what their duty is to their children and how they are to bring them up to God and the fear of Him. If God is willing, we will hear in the next sermon about the office, honor, and obedience of children toward their parents. But so that parents may the more willingly render to their children what God's Word requires of them, they must first consider what a precious treasure they have in the children born to them, since the Holy Spirit

---

5 Hunnius, following the Book of Concord of 1580, adds the phrase from Colossians 3:21, *daß sie nicht scheuw werden*, "that they may not become discouraged," to the citation from Ephesians 6:4.

teaches us in His Word that children are not born without risk, but are given by God Himself, as it is written in Psalm 127: "Children are a gift of the Lord, and the fruit of the womb is a present."

For this reason, at times in the stories about the holy women it is repeated when they become pregnant that the Lord remembered them and gave them the fruit of the womb. They also demonstrated their thankfulness for this with the names they gave their children. When Leah gave birth to her firstborn, she named him Reuben, "for," she said, "the Lord has looked on my affliction." She named her fourth son Judah, "for I want to thank the Lord." Anna named her son Samuel, because "he was requested of the Lord," and so on. The Gospel also teaches us how highly children are regarded with God, for they, as much adults, are to be redeemed with the blood of the Son of God and become heirs of the fellowship of the elect, since they have the special promise of this in Mark 10: "Let the children come to Me and do not hinder them, for of such is the kingdom of heaven." And Matthew 18: "I tell you that their angels in heaven continually see the face of their Father in heaven. For the Son of Man has come to save that which was lost." Therefore Christ also preaches in the same place a powerful sermon to all men, that they should not offend the children in any way: "Whoever receives such a child receives Me. But whoever offends one of the least of these who believe in Me, it would be better for a millstone to be hung around his neck and for him to be drowned in the deepest part of the sea."

Therefore, since they are so highly regarded before God, Christian parents will be all the more willing to fulfill their duty, doing what they ought for their children.

What, then, are their duties? The first is provided by nature and reason itself and is implanted in the human heart: that they are to love their children. For if they didn't love their own children, they would be worse than brute beasts. No animal is so wild and savage that it doesn't love its own young, as experience demonstrates.

Therefore, it is an unchristian thing with some parents when God gives them children and they are dissatisfied with them.

They would rather be rid of them. They become secretly angry with God in their heart for giving them children. When a pestilence or plague strikes and their children are spared, they become impatient about it, wishing that the pestilence would strike down their own children—their own flesh and blood. Such unchristian parents should be directed to the brute beasts. The fierce lions, wolves and bears love their young and have a natural inclination toward them. So parents like these are more merciless than the wolves, lions and bears. Godly parents ought to love their children and follow the example of the heavenly Father in this matter. On account of His great, inexpressible love toward us men, He compares Himself to a father and a mother. He says in Psalm 103: "As a father has compassion on his children, so the Lord has compassion on those who fear Him." And in Isaiah 49: "Can a woman also forget her child so that she fails to have compassion on the son of her womb?"

But just as one can show too little love toward his children, as mentioned, so one can also show too much love for them, so that the parents love their children beyond what is good, and out of a twisted sort of love, they are too permissive, letting them do many things that they should rather warn them against. Indeed, when it is viewed in the right light, this is not a true and proper love, but a twisted love, as we shall hear.

But if fathers or mothers love their children rightly, then the remaining things will follow that much sooner. For in connection with this natural love that is implanted in nature, parents are responsible for maintaining their children so that they have all the sustenance they need. As the Apostle says in 2 Cor. 12: "Children should not lay up treasures for their parents, but the parents for their children."

On the other hand, there are people who do neither too much nor too little for their children, for there are some who pay no attention to their children whatsoever and fail to consider how they might leave something behind for their children. They eat too much, drink too much, and needlessly spend away everything that they might leave as an inheritance. They may well say things like, "If my children want to have anything after I'm gone, then let them earn it themselves!" In this way they see to it, for their part, that their children are turned into beggars, so that they are forced to hang onto other people's necks and be a burden to them. The apostle writes about such people in 1 Timothy 5: "Anyone who will not look after his own is worse than a pagan and has denied the faith."

Then again one finds other people who do far too much for their children in this matter. They work day and night in order to store up great riches and treasures so that they might create a great stockpile of wealth for their children. Therefore, they scratch and scrape together whatever they can, without bothering to ask if they are obtaining it justly or unjustly. They burden their consciences and their own souls over it while imagining that everything will turn out just fine, as long as they set aside a good amount for their children in this world. This is to fall into sin on the other side. Yes, we should work and see to it that our own may be provided for, but we must do it with God and with honor. We should do our part and commit the rest to God. If He gives much, then we must give thanks to Him and ask Him as well that our children may not, through temporal possessions, be turned away from the highest eternal possession. If He gives little, then we should trust God, who gave us children, to know also how to care for them.

Now, this is still the smallest matter, a fleeting thing which only pertains to this life, namely, how children are to be cared for with proper nourishment for their bodies. Parents, because of their office, are responsible for something even more important, namely, for seeing how their children may be brought to heaven and to eternal life, on account of which they were created and for which they were purchased with the blood of the Son of God.

Accordingly, since children are conceived and born in sin and are by nature children of wrath, namely, flesh born of flesh, and since they are shut out of heaven and eternal life due to their unclean, corrupt nature, it should be the primary concern of godly Christian parents that their children, born in this world, are brought as soon as possible to Holy Baptism to be born again of water and the Holy Spirit and incorporated into the Lord Jesus Christ. This is in consideration of the divine ordinance, since God instituted Holy Baptism not only for mature adults, but also for children. As the Lord Christ says: "Unless a person is born again of water and Spirit, he cannot enter into the kingdom of God." And lest one should think, as the Anabaptists falsely interpret the Word of Christ, that Christ is speaking there only of adults, as Nicodemus was at that time, the Lord Christ immediately adds a clear, undeniable interpretation to this word, saying: "That which is born of flesh is flesh," that is, it is sinful and eternally condemned before the judgment seat of God. Therefore, the spiritual rebirth is necessary so that the first, carnal, natural birth may not cause him to lose out on salvation. Now, it is certain beyond doubt and eternally true that children also are flesh born of flesh. Indeed, when does this carnal birth take place? Certainly not when the person has grown into an adult, but in childhood. And that which is born of flesh in childhood should and must be born again. How? "Of water and the Holy Spirit." With "water" Christ understands no other water than that of Holy Baptism, which is for this reason called a washing of rebirth and renewal of the Holy Spirit (Titus 3).

Since, then, the parents are under the earnest order and command of the Lord Christ, they should not postpone for long the Baptism of the children God has granted to them. Rather, since Baptism is available to them as soon as they are born, they should also hasten to it immediately and in no way be delayed to their great peril.

It is indeed a wicked, unchristian practice when people sometimes allow the poor children to lie unbaptized for several weeks simply because they are busy preparing a meal.

To be sure, there is a place for Christian meals after such an event. These are not forbidden of themselves. We read that

Abraham held a great banquet on the day when his son Isaac was weaned. But that Baptism should wait for the meal, so that that which is necessary waits for that which is unnecessary—that is a twisted and foolish work that is not to be tolerated. One can allow the Baptism to go forward, since God's Son makes it so important, and spare the meal for another occasion (if one wants to make it a grand event that requires much preparation and time), as the example of Abraham practically encourages. He did not set up this banquet on the day of Isaac's circumcision, much less did he postpone the circumcision for the sake of it, but he had the circumcision of his son go forward at the time set by God, and spared the meal until the day of his weaning.

Godly parents should follow this example of the father of all believers and bring their children to Holy Baptism as soon after their birth as possible, that they may be devoted to God, be recorded in the Book of Life, become citizens of the elect congregation of God, be buried there into the death of Christ, and rise to a new, divine life (Rom. 6).

But once this is done, still more is required of parents, that they order and arrange everything to the highest degree so that their children may be preserved in this covenant of grace to eternal life. For although this is a work of God, nevertheless He uses the discipline of the parents to this end as a salutary means. It is their duty, as soon as their children begin to talk, to get them accustomed to prayer, that they may call upon their heavenly Father with their tender mouth. Such a prayer is most pleasing to God the Lord, as He who is wont to ordain strength from the mouth of young children and nursing babes (as He attests in the eighth Psalm), regardless of the fact that young babes still do not understand what they are asking. For since God does not even despise the cry of the young ravens when they cry to Him, in their own way, for food, according to the statement of Scripture (Job 39, Psalm 147), how much more should the childish prayers of the dear little children of God be pleasing to Him? After all, they have been purchased at a high price with the blood of His dear Son, Jesus Christ, and made children of the heavenly Father in Holy Baptism. Therefore, God often regards the prayer of the children and blesses the parents and even the entire household on their account.

But there are also found all kinds of failures and deficiencies in this area. There are many coarse parents who let their children grow up like brute beasts. They do not train them up in prayer, nor in the Catechism, nor in children's instruction, nor in any exercise of godliness, even though this is one of the most important parts of the duty of parents to their children. They have an express commandment to do this in the words of the holy apostle Paul: "Parents, bring up your children in the training and admonition of the Lord." Indeed, how earnestly Moses, that great prophet and man of God, commanded this to all parents in Deuteronomy 6: "These words that I am commanding you today you shall take to heart, and you shall teach them to your children." The Holy Spirit explains the same thing in Psalm 78: "He established a testimony in Jacob, and gave a law in Israel, that He commanded our fathers to teach to their children, so that the next generation should learn, and the children who have not yet been born, when they arise, might also announce it to their children, that they set their hope on God and not forget the deeds of God; that they might keep His commandments."

With these words, the Spirit of God has not only elucidated for us the commandment pertaining to parents in this respect, but at the same time He has also clarified the benefit that follows such training when children are encouraged to pray and God's Word is embedded in their yet little understanding, namely, that they are thereby raised to fear God, to set their hope on Him, and to keep His commandments.

When God had determined to destroy the land of Sodom with fire and brimstone on account of the wickedness of its inhabitants, He wanted to speak about it first with Abraham. He said: "How can I hide from Abraham what I am doing, since he shall become a great and powerful people, and all peoples on earth shall be blessed in him? For I know," God says, "that he will command his children and his house after him to keep the way of the Lord and to do what is right and good." According to this example, every father should be a preacher in his own home, who depicts well for his children and implants in them from childhood on whatever serves to awaken a right, true fear of God in their hearts.

The godly man Tobias diligently admonishes his son to keep God before his eyes throughout his entire life, to guard against sin, to give to the poor and needy gladly and willingly, to beware of harlotry and pride, to thank God at all times, and to pray that he may follow God's Word and commandments in all his undertakings (Tob. 4).

If parents these days would show similar diligence in admonishing their children in the Lord and bringing them up with discipline, oh, how much better all things in the world would be than they sadly are at present!

If they really want it to go well with their children and keep them safe from the hangman here on earth and from the devil hereafter, then they will surely allow nothing to get in the way of such discipline, training and instruction. For this is true, fatherly love of which we spoke above. He who loves his child disciplines him. For this reason Solomon writes: "Do not fail to discipline the young child. For if you strike him with rods, it will not kill him. You are striking him with rods, but you are saving his soul from hell."

Why is it that so many disobedient people must be punished by the executioner? A common reason is that they lacked Christian discipline in their youth, and their parents let them grow up in complete wantonness and allowed them to be confirmed in wickedness. Since they were not hindered from sin and vice with the rod, the executioner has to take care of them with the sword, and the parents clap their hands together over their heads in terrible, heartfelt sorrow for their flesh and blood when they are forced to deal with the reality of their great permissiveness, and how wickedly they acted in not using the rod to the full, and in failing to lead their children to the fear of the Lord. In addition to the heartfelt sorrow they experience over their children, they also have a bad conscience, like a gnawing worm in the bosom, that by their own fault their children were so poorly counseled, and they (the parents) must one day stand before the Judge of the living and the dead and answer for it. For God also plans to judge such pernicious, shameful permissiveness in the parents, both temporally and, if they do not apologize to Him for it during the time of grace, also eternally.

It is well known how it went for the priest Eli, who had two sons with whom he was far too lenient. He spared them from discipline. Therefore, they grew up in their own wantonness. They became crude, secure and godless, and they behaved shamefully before all Israel. Their father let everything go and, as the story tells us, never once became angry with them. And even when he did say something to them about their vices and wicked behavior, it was far too mild. For this reason, our Lord God finally imposed this penalty, that father and sons would die on the same day. (We read about this in 1 Samuel 3 and 4.) It is especially noteworthy that, when the Lord God has Eli the priest rebuked for his terribly twisted permissiveness, He has it pointed out to him, among other things: "You honored your children more than Me," in order to get him to understand how gravely the Almighty God views this sin, as God is dishonored by it and men are loved and honored more than Himself, even though He is to be loved, feared, and honored above all things.

Therefore it also follows that parents and children are punished with one another, and when the children grow up, they hang on the throat and neck of their parents, behave disobediently in all things, and grieve them mightily. Along these lines there is an especially handsome reminder in the book of Sirach, chapter 30, contained in these words: "A spoiled child is willful as a horse. Pamper your child, and you will have to fear him from then on. Play with him, and he will grieve you ever after. Do not joke around with him, lest you have to mourn over him thereafter and gnash your teeth in the end. Do not let him do whatever he wants in his youth, and do not make excuses for his foolishness. Bend his neck while he is still young. Bruise his back while he is still little, so that he does not become stiff-necked and disobedient to you." Now that is what you call a stern and proper warning for parents not to be too lenient with their children, as it expressly portrays the filth, disobedience, trouble and pain that results from it.

On the other hand, those who raise their children for instruction and admonition in the Lord in accord with the apostolic reminder experience joy in them. As it is written in the Proverbs of Solomon, chapter 29: "Discipline your son, and he will delight you and give rest to your soul." And Sirach says in the aforementioned chapter: "Whoever loves his child keeps him ever under the rod, that he may thereafter have joy in him. Whoever keeps his child in discipline will rejoice over him and will not be ashamed of him with his acquaintances. If a man disciplines his child, he thwarts his enemy and gladdens his friend. For if his father dies, it is as if he had not died, for he has left his likeness behind him. If he lives, he sees his desire and rejoices in it. If he dies, he has nothing to worry about, for he has left behind a defense against his enemy, one who can continue to serve his friends."

But just as no diligence is to be spared in the discipline of home and children and in Christian instruction in the fear and reverence of God, so also it becomes all the more necessary that the parents themselves set a fine, noble, inoffensive pattern of living for their children. For how can the discipline of the parents benefit the children if they themselves are incorrigible, if the children are exposed to all sorts of coarse sins and must daily watch as their parents live in disharmony, berate and revile one another, blaspheme God, neglect preaching, care nothing for God's Word or the holy Sacraments, lie around all day long, covet and practice usury and do other such things? In this way they ruin and destroy everything that they otherwise could have done to benefit their children. For this reason and for the sake of their children, they should also restrain themselves from such offensive behavior so that their children are not caused to stumble by it. For otherwise they will be heaping twice the guilt upon themselves, since the Lord Christ so strictly forbids anyone to cause the little children to stumble (Mat. 18) and clearly signals that if anyone does so, it would be better for a millstone to be hung around his neck and for him to be drowned in the deepest part of the sea.

To be sure, even where no such offense is given, experience teaches how difficult it is for children to be preserved in the fear of God—even when their parents expend all possible diligence in doing so. The dear patriarchs undoubtedly left nothing out, insofar as they were able, and yet they, too, had unruly children. Adam had the murderer Cain. Noah had wicked Ham. Abraham, that mocker Ishmael. Isaac, the savage Esau. Jacob, the unruly sons Simeon and Levi, together with the rest who conspired in their bloodthirsty council against godly, innocent Joseph to kill him. And when their plot was thwarted, they sold him into slavery in Egypt. Samuel, too, was an especially holy prophet and man of God, who undoubtedly spared no diligence in disciplining his children. And yet his two sons, Joel and Abdias, did not behave well. They were supposed to be judges, but they were covetous and accepted bribes and perverted justice. David, too, had several children who were good for nothing, as we see in Amnon, Absalom and Adonijah.

Now, if this was the case for the greatest and holiest of men who both applied salutary instruction and set an example of good, inoffensive behavior for their children, what will be the case when the parents themselves are crude and wicked? Therefore godly Christian parents will take this to heart and will be careful not to put any stumbling block before their children by leading an evil, sinful life, or by omitting anything from their instruction.

But just as, with some, these matters are handled with too much laxity, so one finds others who strike their children too hard and deal with them too harshly, who punish their children with anger and bitterness whenever they imagine that they have sinned, who are unable to practice discipline with moderation. Children are not improved by this. On the contrary, some become dreadful and ugly through it. They do not know how they are supposed to act in order to earn the thanks or to avoid the ire of their parents. Some get it in their heads that, if their parents can become angry, then the children, too, can become angry and complain, so that nothing comes of it except for a purely ill-mannered, wild, and contumacious existence. Naturally one must be earnest in the discipline of the children and should not deal with them too tenderly, as stated above. But there is a certain balance to everything. Too little and too much ruins the whole game, as they say. St. Paul did not write in vain to the Ephesians: "Fathers, do not provoke your children to anger." Nor does the Wisdom of Solomon, which requires the discipline of children, miss the mark when it prescribes that there be a goal and a balance to it. For it says: "Discipline your son while there is hope, but let not your soul be moved to kill him. For great fury brings harm. Therefore, let him be. Then you can discipline him later." Saul was like a ferocious lion in his house in this matter; he threw his spear at his own son Jonathan, who had done nothing wrong, but only properly defended the innocent man David to his father (1 Sam. 20). He also wanted to have him killed when he ate some honey in the woods (1 Sam. 14), although Jonathan knew nothing about his father's prohibition or the threat attached to it. He would have done it, if the people hadn't intervened and saved godly Jonathan from the hand of his father. These people are called "unloving" in the Scriptures, people who suppress the natural affection, love and inclination toward their children and behave tyrannically with them. But this should not be, according to St. Paul and Solomon, as we have now considered from their testimonies.

But the office of parents also extends to include, along with the inner fear of God and the outward discipline, that they raise their children to carry on an honorable craft, trade or skill, so that they do not grow accustomed to idleness, from which nothing but poverty and ruin follow, as Solomon teaches us in Proverbs chapters 6, 10, 19, 20 and 28.

And then, when their children grow up and reach a marriageable age, parents are to see to it that they help their children to marry, seeking for them a Christian spouse who is pious and God-fearing and keeps the pure, unadulterated doctrine and faith from the heart. In this matter, not only fleeting temporal goods, but especially discipline, godliness, and respectability are at stake, which is the best reward of all, so that children may ever after be endowed with these things. This is what Abraham, the father of all believers, did when he wanted to find a wife for his son Isaac. He made his servant swear an oath that he would not take a wife for him from the daughters of the unbelieving Canaanites, but would go to his father's house and bring back for his son Isaac a woman who was of his kindred, confession and faith, even as it came to pass. Among these concerns, parents must consider the great danger if they find spouses for their children who are not of the right, pure faith and confession, lest the believer be easily led astray. Indeed, the children who are born to them are placed in the utmost danger of being misled. This happened even to the wise King Solomon when he consorted with foreign idol-worshiping women, so that he himself finally fell into idolatry through them. Therefore great vigilance is required.

May the merciful God, who is the true Father over all that is called "children" in heaven and on earth, deign to teach parents their duty in the governing of the home, and may He grant them grace to raise their children in holy fear and obedience to Him, so that parents and children may, with one accord, praise God and the Lord Jesus Christ, here in time and there in eternity. Amen.

Seventh Sermon on the Table of Duties: Children

Ephesians 6

Children, be obedient to your parents in the Lord. For this is right: Honor father and mother—which is the first commandment that has a promise—that it may go well for you and you may live long on the earth.

In the Table of Duties, dear friends in Christ, we have before us the third estate or domain, which is and is called the domestic estate. And we have recently learned about the vocation and duty of parents toward children. On this occasion the children's lesson must be held before them so that they understand what they, in turn, ought to do and how they are to behave when it comes to their parents.

But this part of the Table of Duties properly belongs under the Fourth of the Holy Ten Commandments. Therefore the apostle Paul also explains the duty of children with reference to that commandment when he says in the words that were just read: "Children, be obedient to your parents in the Lord. For this is right: Honor father and mother, etc."

The apostle then adds two parts to this: First, what children owe their parents, and then, what should motivate them to do this. By the grace of God, we intend to treat each of these parts separately.

Part One: What Children Owe Their Parents

What is it that children should do for their parents? First, since Christ summed up all the commandments in these two commandments—You shall love your Lord God with all your heart, with all your soul, with all your mind, and with all your strength; and your neighbor as yourself, so that love toward God is commanded in the First Table of the Ten Commandments and love toward the neighbor in the Second—it follows that, since the Fourth Commandment pertains to the Second Table, children owe their parents genuine love. For next to God, no one is closer to children than their parents from whom they were born and from whom, next to God, they have received life. So it is that this love for the parents is instilled in human nature. From this all the rest of the duties that follow flow forth, as from a spring, and remain with the children, together with love.

Ruth is a model to all children of this love. The Scriptures praise her, recounting how deeply she loved her mother-in-law (who served as a mother to her), such that, when her mother-in-law Naomi wanted to leave the territory of the Moabites and return to the land of Israel, Ruth followed after her and absolutely refused to be driven away from her. "Do not tell me to forsake you," she says, "or to turn away from you. Where you go, I also shall go. Where you stay, I also shall stay. Your people is my people, and your God is my God. Where you die, I also shall die; there shall I also be buried. The Lord do this and that to me if anything but death separates me and you."

In the papacy the matter is completely turned upside down; it is actually considered a special service to God when children shrug off their parents, hide away in a monastery, and, by virtue of their invented rules, never see their parents again. In so doing, they have tried to earn heaven, even as they suppress the natural love that God has implanted in them, contrary to the Fourth Commandment, and, as Christ accuses the Pharisees in a similar situation, trample the commandment of God for the sake of a human tradition (Mat. 15). How ridiculous, when the very first thing that God requires of children is that they love their parents!

In addition to love, God also requires in the same commandment honor, that they hold their parents in all honor, both inwardly and outwardly. Inwardly, to be sure, so that they truly think well of their parents and honor them in their hearts, recognizing that God Himself has placed them in their children's lives and wants them to be honored according to His good ordinance. But they are also to be honored outwardly, so that children should behave humbly and decently and live under the supervision of their earthly parents with due outward obedience. "A son shall indeed honor his father," as Malachi has written in the first chapter.

This command to honor parents is never lifted, even if God places the children in a higher estate, with greater riches, power, dignity and glory than their parents have. Solomon was indeed elevated to a position of such glory, power, wisdom, praise, fame and admiration before all the peoples on earth—as much as anyone could possibly attain. Nevertheless, even in this supreme royal majesty of his, he did not forget the Fourth Commandment. He remained conscious of the fact that, in spite of his majesty, he was still obliged to honor father and mother. Therefore, when on one occasion, as the story goes, his mother Bathsheba came to ask him for something, King Solomon got up, went to meet her, bowed down—that is, bent down to the ground humbly before her, and had her throne placed at his right hand, and thus received her with special homage.

Who was more glorious in his day than the great prophet and man of God Moses? And yet when his father-in-law Jethro (who was a father to Moses) came to him, Moses bowed down before him and showed him all honor, in spite of the fact that he didn't compare to Moses in gifts, wisdom and dignity (Exo. 18). This was not a dishonorable thing for either Moses or Solomon to do, and it brought no shame to them in their great dignity and majesty. On the contrary, it is much more to their credit and glory that these things were caused to be written by the Holy Spirit.

Thirdly, children owe their parents obedience and are obliged to obey them in everything that is in accord with and not contrary to God's Word, truth, righteousness, and decency. For if they should command something that is ungodly, one must obey

God rather than men. In the same way, Jonathan, the son of King Saul, was unwilling to follow his father's bloodthirsty commandment when he ordered him to bring in David, the son of Jesse, in order that he should be put to death (1 Sam. 20). But otherwise, when father and mother command what is decent, Christian, good, and right—something that can be performed by children with a good conscience—then children are bound by God's Word to be obedient to them. "Obey your father who raised you," says Solomon in Proverbs 23. And it is written in the third chapter of Sirach: "Whatever a mother calls on her children to do, God would see it done."

No one should consider himself too old for this. For even Moses was not ashamed to follow the advice of his father-in-law Jethro when he counseled him about how he should handle matters so that the whole burden of ruling did not rest on him alone. So we see, too, in the example of godly Isaac how he was obedient to his father, as the account in Genesis 22 describes it. When he thought he would be sacrificed, he patiently allowed himself to be bound and willingly surrendered in obedience to his father Abraham. How difficult that must have been for him according to the flesh!

This obedience lasts as long as the parents are alive, and is required most of all when the children want to get married, so that they do not enter into a marriage secretly or behind the backs of their dear parents, without their foreknowledge and approval. Sadly, many disobedient children secretly get engaged to persons about whom they have told their parents nothing beforehand, having neither listened to their advice nor waited for their approval. Parents are often terribly grieved by this, and such children cause their parents dreadful heartache, as Rebecca mourned over Esau when he had taken wives from the daughters of Canaan. She said: "It pains me to live on account of the daughters of Heth," whom Esau had taken for himself (Genesis 27).

Godly children are, in this matter, as in other proper matters, obliged to obey their dear parents. Isaac followed his father's wishes and took for a wife the woman whom Abraham had sent his house steward Eleazer to bring back for him, regardless of the fact that Isaac had neither seen nor known her beforehand (Gen. 24). Jacob followed the behest of his parents who sent him to their kindred in Mesopotamia to take a wife there (Gen. 28).

And, to be sure, when their children secretly get engaged, parents must assert their rights, and, insofar as they have serious reasons to prevent still greater mischief, can hinder and reverse this illegitimate, secret engagement. In such a case, too, children are bound to abide by their parents' will, so that they recognize the wrong they have done and leave it to father and mother to decide if they will affirm such a disorderly marriage arrangement with their future consent and approval, or if they will object to it. The children are, for the moment, still under the authority of their parents. For it was expressly commanded in the Law of Moses that, if a virgin made a vow while she was still living in her father's house, and her father, on the day he heard of it, objected to it and took exception to it, then neither the vow nor the contract was binding, because her father took exception to it. Children should take away from this that disorderly, secret vows in matters pertaining to marriage are even less binding if father and mother, for urgent reasons, are not willing to accept it. But in such a case, the parents must proceed wisely and prudently, as pointed out on another occasion, so that an even greater judgment may not follow, as experience so often demonstrates.

Fourthly, children owe their fathers and mothers patience. For this is how the teacher Sirach teaches and instructs children: "Honor father and mother with deeds, with words, and with patience," namely, so that they bear patiently with the faults and shortcomings of their parents, as much as can be done with a good conscience, especially when they are old, incapacitated, and even act strangely and harshly at times—something that often accompanies old age. In these cases, it is proper for pious, God-fearing children to cover up the faults of their parents, following the example of Shem and Japheth (Gen. 9). "Think kindly of your father, even if he acts like a child, and do not despise him because you are more skillful than he" (Sirach 3).

But one notes in this a great fault among many children; they are unwilling to be forbearing with their father and mother. From this there often springs an irreconcilable envy and hatred, a constant strife and discord among those who, on account of God and of nature, are the most closely related to one another.

God's Word also requires, fifthly, that children should care for their parents, see to it that they are fed and nourished, and, as Paul teaches, "repay them" (1 Tim. 5), especially when they become so old, poor and weak that they can no longer acquire food for themselves. Sirach again preaches about this, saying: "Dear child, take care of your father when he is old, and do not grieve him as long as he lives." When Jacob suffered want during a time of famine, his obedient, God-fearing son Joseph came to his aid, and provided for him and took care of him for the rest of his life (Gen. 47).

Ruth provided food for her mother-in-law by the work of her hand (Ruth 2). David followed the same pattern in caring for his father and mother and providing refuge for them in the land of the Moabites, since they couldn't be entirely safe from King Saul in the land of Judah (1 Sam. 22). Indeed, Christ Himself cared for His dear mother and commanded His disciple John to take charge of her care (John 19).

But experience shows how poorly many children carry out this duty of theirs. It is as the proverb says: "It is far easier for one father to provide for ten children than for ten children to provide for one father." It takes too much effort to care for the parents, so that one becomes tired of them, and Satan thus blots out natural love from the hearts of many wicked children, so that they secretly (and occasionally also expressly and openly) wish death upon their parents, simply so that they no longer have to be burdened with them. They think so little of their parents that they make life bitter for them, even though they ought to be a crutch to them in their old age, as Hannah, the mother of Tobias, calls her son a comfort in her old age. We will discuss later how things turn out for such perverse children.

In the sixth and last place, it also behooves children, when God calls their earthly parents out of this life and takes them from this passing world, to mourn for them properly and to respectfully commit them to the ground. Tobias, when he was old, entrusted this to his son in a solemn testament, saying to him: "Dear son, hear my words and hold them fast in your heart. When God takes my soul away, then bury my body. Also," he goes on to say, "after your mother dies, then bury her next to me." In the same way, Isaac and Ishmael buried their father; Jacob and Esau buried Isaac; Joseph and his brothers buried their father Jacob. Indeed, this is the final honor that children can show to their dear parents.

All of this, then, is required of children, as has been demonstrated, and if they do it, they show themselves to be godly children who honor their father and mother according to the Fourth Commandment.

But since, as noted, children often fail to perform the duties we have recounted, in order that they may the more willingly show the love, honor, obedience, patience and benevolence that is required of them and the more diligently guard themselves from disobedience and what pertains to it, we will now also take up the reasons that should motivate children faithfully to carry out their duty as children.

Part Two: What Should Motivate Children

First of all, if they had no other reason to honor their parents besides God's Word and commandment, "You shall honor your father and mother," that would still be reason enough. Paul intends to lead them to this disposition when he writes: "They shall be obedient to their parents in the Lord," that is, in the fear of the Lord and on account of His commandment. For since God commands it, it follows that whoever does not honor father and mother is being disobedient to the mouth of the Lord and is breaking His immutable commandment. Thus we are not dealing here with men only, but with the living God, who is a strict and jealous God toward all those who intentionally and contemptuously transgress His commandments.

But not only is it something that God commands in His Word and Law; it is also "right," says St. Paul. That is, it is required and accompanied also by the light of nature, common sense, natural law, and by the sense of uprightness and justice implanted in the heart of men, that men are obliged to honor and submit to those from whom, next to God, they have their life.

Therefore the heathen also have had to recognize this by the indwelling light of their reason, and accordingly they have commanded the obedience of children toward their parents while earnestly punishing disobedience.

The holy teacher Sirach points to this fundamental reason in chapter 7: "Honor your father with your whole heart, and do not forget how much labor you caused for your mother. Remember that you were born from them. Indeed, what can you do for them in return for what they have done for you?" And what the Spirit of God teaches there in general, the godly old Tobias pointed out to his young son in his aforementioned testament with these words: "Honor your mother all your life long. Remember the danger she withstood when she carried you under her heart."

The precious promise that God has attached to this commandment should also make the children all the more desirous, willing, and diligent to keep it. St. Paul expressly emphasizes this, namely: "Honor your father and mother. This is the first commandment that has a promise—that it may go well with you and you may live long on the earth." There is no promise so expressly and clearly added to the other commandments as there is to this one. This, according to St. Paul's interpretation, was not done in vain; it was added in order to point out to all children how well-pleasing obedience to parents is to our Lord and God, since it is something that He will not permit to go unrewarded, but sees to it that obedient children also enjoy the rewards of their obedience in this world, so that they should live long and it should go well with them on the earth.

The Holy Spirit, in the divine Scriptures, has drawn several admonitions from this promise for the sole purpose of depicting for children what such Christian obedience looks like. Sirach 3: "God will not punish the sin of the one who honors his father, and he who honors his mother will collect a great reward. He who honors his father will also have joy in his children, and when he prays, he will be heard. He who honors his father will live that much longer." And shortly afterward, in the same chapter, he writes: "Honor your father and mother, so that their blessing may come upon you. For the blessing of a father builds the children's homes." That is, it brings good fortune, health, and well-being to the home, so that they are blessed in their domestic affairs. Again Sirach says: "He who shows kindness to his father will never be forgotten." So it is that the wise King Solomon included this promise in his Proverbs and expands on it with his own example in chapter 4, saying: "I was also my father's son, tender, and the only one before my mother. And he taught me and said, 'Let your heart be attentive to my words. Keep my commandment and you will live. Accept wisdom. Accept understanding. Do not forget it, and do not depart from the speech of my mouth. Do not forsake it, and it will preserve you. Love it, and it will protect you.'"

God does not let this promise remain a matter of empty words; He fulfills it powerfully and has set before us the example of the Scriptures in order to demonstrate the certainty of His divine assertion. Shem and Japheth honored their father, and it went well with them on the earth (Gen. 9). Isaac was obedient to his father, and he was richly rewarded for it by God (Gen. 22). When Rebecca obeyed her dear parents and went to fetch water, God marvelously bestowed on her the good fortune of becoming Isaac's wife and a grandmother of the Lord Christ (Gen. 24). When Saul went to look for his father's lost donkeys, he found a kingdom. For it was through this very insignificant errand that he came to the prophet Samuel, who, by divine mandate, anointed him king over the people of God (1 Sam. 9-10). While David, in obedience to his father Jesse, was out tending to the sheep, the lot fell to him that he should be anointed king over the whole people of Israel (1 Sam. 16). Also at another time when he was sent by his father into the Israelite camp to bring all sorts of food items to his brothers, it turned out that, through that very encounter he ended up fighting with and defeating the uncircumcised Philistine Goliath. The Lord thus brought about through him a great aid and deliverance for all Israel (1 Sam. 17). In a similar way, young Tobias' obedience as a child to his father and mother was richly rewarded, so that it went well for him and he lived a long life on the earth.

But God especially made good on His promise attached to the Fourth Commandment with regard to the Rechabites. The Rechabites had received a command from their father Jonadab, the son of Rechab, that neither they nor their descendants should drink wine, nor build houses, nor sow seed, nor plant vineyards, but should live their entire lives in tents, so that they might live long in the land in which they sojourned. This was a strict commandment and extremely difficult to keep. Nevertheless, they were so obedient to the ordinance of their father that, when the prophet Jeremiah, at God's bidding, set wine before them to drink (so that He might use this example to punish the disobedience of the Jews all the more), they would not drink or turn aside from the bidding of their father, but obeyed in all that he had commanded them. Therefore the Lord made this promise to the house of the Rechabites: "Thus says the Lord of hosts, the God of Israel: Because you have obeyed the commandment of your father Jonadab and have kept all his commandments and done all that he commanded you, therefore, thus says the Lord of hosts, the God of Israel: Jonadab, the son of Rechab, shall never fail to have someone standing before Me at all times." There we hear how highly pleased God is by the obedience that Christian children show to their parents, and how truly they will have and find His sure reward for it. He gives us this example so that children may also be enticed by it to honor and obey their father and mother.

Thus it is also in itself a special blessing to children, so that the wise King Solomon compares such obedience to a beautiful, glorious ornament, as he writes in his Proverbs: "My child, obey the instruction of your father, and do not forsake the commandment of your mother. For it is a beautiful ornament for your head, and a garland around your neck."

But since children are often unsatisfied with the promise of kindness, God has not only revealed in His Word how pleasing obedience is to Him and how richly He wishes to reward it. He has also demonstrated what a cursed and shameful vice disobedience is, and what punishment children earn for themselves when they oppose their earthly parents in word or deed.

Solomon's wisdom again explains for us what we are to think of such disobedient children in Proverbs 19: "He who mistreats his father and chases away his mother is a shameful and cursed child." Sirach confirms this when he writes: "To despise your mother is your own shame." Therefore these children are reckoned to be under the wicked, crude generation that Solomon speaks of in Proverbs 30.

It is for this reason that God also threatens them with great harm. As it is written in Exodus 21: "He who strikes his father or mother shall be put to death." Likewise: "He who curses his father or mother shall be put to death." God wanted this to be so deeply impressed on the people of Israel that, in Deuteronomy 21, He commanded that, if a father has a stubborn, disobedient son who does not obey the voice of his father and mother, and if, after they discipline him, he still refuses to listen to them, then his father and mother should take hold of him, bring him to the elders of the city, and show them that their son is disobedient, a glutton, and a drunkard. Then all the people of that city should stone him to death right then and there, so that all Israel may hear and be afraid.

There are many more of these testimonies of the Holy Spirit concerning the punishment of disobedient children. It is written: "He who curses his father or mother shall have his lamp extinguished in the midst of darkness" (Pro. 20). Likewise: "He who forsakes his father will be put to shame, and whoever grieves his mother is cursed by the Lord" (Sirach 3). And again: "The eye of the one who mocks his father and hates to obey his mother must be plucked out by the ravens near the brook and eaten by the young eagles" (Pro. 30).

Now, we should not imagine that these are merely frightening words. It is the Holy Spirit who speaks and announces these things, who neither lies nor is able to lie. And experience itself proves this, confirming for us with daily, clear examples that such disobedient children rarely die of natural causes. God reveals His judgment upon them—that they are handed over to the hangman and have their eyes plucked out by the ravens as a frightful and terrifying example to others, so that they may guard themselves from similar disobedience. The wicked child Ham had to be cursed, together with all his descendants, for dishonoring his father (Gen. 9). How did things turn out for Abimelech? He repaid his father with evil for all his fatherly faithfulness by slaughtering seventy of his father's children on a stone, although they were his own half-brothers (Judges 9). But misfortune finally caught up with him, so that his lamp was treacherously extinguished. For he was fatally wounded by a woman with a millstone and was pierced through by his own servant. The Holy Spirit adds these noteworthy words to the end of his story: "Thus God repaid Abimelech for the evil that he had done to his father when he slaughtered his seventy brothers."

But God demonstrated His wrath and fury even more dreadfully in the case of the cursed son Absalom. He chased his father away, seized the land for himself, raped his concubines in broad daylight, and set out against his father with the force of an army in order to apprehend him and take the life of him from whom, next to God, he had received life. But God caused the army of his father David to be victorious, and He gave Absalom over to the curse of being hanged on a tree by his own hair and pierced through with a spear; his life had to end in misery. It is to be understood that his poor soul was also forfeit.

Thus the lesson remains that God wishes to bring dreadful punishment upon children for their great and shameful thanklessness and rebellion toward their father and mother, both temporally and (if they do not repent) also eternally. For, if evil shall not leave the house of the one who repays another man evil for good (Pro. 17), how much less can misfortune turn aside from those who are thankless toward their own parents, who have spent so much anguish, care, trouble and labor on them, including having brought their children into the world and raised them from infancy.

Therefore, in order that children may enjoy God's favor and benefit from His pledge and promise that it may go well with them on the earth, and also that they may escape terrible punishment (which, through the judgment of the Holy Scriptures, comes upon all wicked, stubborn, selfish and rebellious children), they will love their parents from the heart, honor them, and listen to them. They will, as much as possible, willingly do everything that is good and fitting for upright, godly, Christian children. In this way they will not only enjoy the favor and blessing of their earthly parents, but they will also have God Himself as a gracious Father for Christ's sake, who will be most kindly disposed toward them and will care for them as a Father both temporally and eternally. To Him be glory, honor and praise, forever and ever. Amen.

Eighth Sermon on the Table of Duties: Menservants and Maidservants

Ephesians 6

Slaves, be obedient to your earthly masters, with fear and trembling, in sincerity of heart, as to Christ, not only serving before their eyes, as if to please men, but as servants of Christ, so that you do the will of God from the heart, with goodwill. Remember that you serve the Lord, not men, knowing that whatever good anyone does, he will receive the same from the Lord, whether he is a slave or a free man.

Beloved in the Lord, since we have sufficiently grasped the content of the third part of the Christian Table of Duties (which deals with domestic governance) with regard to the duty of husbands and wives toward one another and parents and children toward one another, we now come to the third order in the domestic estate, which is that of masters and mistresses toward menservant and maidservants, and then of menservants and maidservants toward their masters and mistresses. In this sermon, we wish to deal with the office, vocation, and assigned tasks of menservants and maidservants, so that they not only know what is proper for them to do and to leave undone in their estate, but also that they may put it into practice.

First, to be sure, although their estate is practically the lowest, they should not imagine that they are more despised before God on account of their low estate. For God does not judge as the children of men judge, nor are His thoughts the thoughts of men (Isa. 55). Yes, with men a master is greater than a servant. But with God (that which pertains to the spiritual, heavenly, and eternal) there is no partiality. As it is written: "In Christ Jesus there is neither Jew nor Greek, neither master nor servant, neither male nor female, but they are altogether one in Christ" (Gal. 3). Thus God also has this characteristic: that He likes to show favor to lowly persons, such as slaves and menservants and maidservants, as Psalm 113 teaches: "Who is like the Lord our God, who has set Himself so high, and yet looks upon the lowly in heaven and on earth?"

In addition, God the Lord created the servant just as much as He created the master, says Job in chapter 13; He has given a body and a rational soul and the breath of life to them both. Christ, likewise, has purchased the manservant and the maidservant with His precious blood just as much as He has purchased the master and the mistress. For these reasons, St. Paul wrote concerning bondservants (as they existed in former times among the heathen) in 1 Cor. 7: "He who is called in the Lord a bondservant is the Lord's freed man."

What is more, Christ Himself was not ashamed to be a servant; He took on the form of a servant, behaved like a servant, and performed the lowly service of a servant for His disciples in washing their feet. Indeed, He served all of us men at once, even purchasing us for eternal life and carrying out the work of our redemption. As He said: "The Son of Man did not come to be served, but to serve, and to give His life as the ransom for many" (Mat. 20). In this way He has, in Himself, dignified and sanctified the lowly servant-estate of menservants and maidservants.

We shall also hear later on that there have been many godly, decent, and noble people who were servants, and yet this was neither an impediment to their proper status nor much less to their salvation. Nor, for that matter, is anyone hindered in his salvation, as long as they perform in their estate what is fitting and proper for them to do on account of the vocation they have received, of which we will now hear further.

To begin with, menservants and maidservants owe their masters and mistresses honor, as it is written in Malachi 1: "A son should honor his father, and a servant his master." They should honor them, that is, they should recognize them as God's good ordinance, under whose protection He has placed them and toward whom He has required obedience.

Accordingly, it behooves them to be faithful and loving to their masters and mistresses in reasonable, godly matters, including risking their lives for them and not forsaking them in danger. Jonathan, the son of Saul, had such a faithful servant in his armorbearer. For when Jonathan, moved by his godly zeal, wanted to attack the Philistine army that was at that time encamped on the field against Israel, he spoke thus to his armorbearer: "Come, let us go over to the camp of these uncircumcised men. Perhaps the Lord will accomplish something through us, for it is not hard for the Lord to help by many or by few." His armorbearer replied: "Do all that is in your heart. Go forth. I am with you, as your heart desires" (1 Sam. 14).

We read about Abra, the maidservant of the widow Judith, how she stayed with her mistress in time of danger, accompanying her into the camp of Holofernes. Menservants and maidservants should display similar faithfulness when their masters and mistresses are in danger, especially when their death draws near, when either their masters or their masters' children are in jeopardy. Then they will by no means withdraw from them before the agreed upon goal has been reached, nor will they abandon them in their time of need. But they will be willing to stay with them, to wait on them properly, and to hold their hand in their pain and sadness. That is their legitimate vocation. They should not abandon it, walking away from their commitment for the sake of their own pleasure, especially when their masters need their service most, being unable quickly to obtain other servants, given the circumstances.

And just as they should stay by the side of their masters in danger, so they are also duty-bound to warn them of danger, as much as possible, and in every way to prove their piety and value by preventing their harm. For that is what it means to be faithful and loving. We read in 1 Samuel 25 how the foolish, immoderate Nabal denied the request of David's envoys with terribly coarse and hostile words, giving them none of the provisions they requested. In doing this, he placed himself and his whole household in grave danger; he should have known that David might attack him and count such overtly merciless behavior against him. But Nabal had a servant who informed his mistress Abigail, Nabal's wife, about the imminent danger and warned her of it. At the urging of her servant, she then provided the means by which the calamity was avoided. This was to the praise of the servant, that he, according to his duty, displayed such faithfulness to his master and mistress. Similarly praiseworthy was the maidservant of the leprous commander Naaman of Syria. She was taken away from the land of Israel and became his slave. But she revealed to him by what means he could be freed of his leprosy, namely, through the help of the prophet in Samaria, Elisha. And later, his menservants also did him a faithful service after the prophet told him that if he bathed seven times in the Jordan, he would be cleansed of his leprosy. He was unwilling to do it, but his servants entreated him with faithful admonition, saying: "Dear father, if the prophet had called on you to do something great, wouldn't you have done it?" Thus they urged him to go through with it, and he was cleansed of his leprosy (2 Kings 5).

God's Word lays out for servants what other tasks, service, and performance are required of them: that they should be obedient, working diligently and carrying out without complaint what they are ordered to do. And they should do this with proper fear, from the bottom of their heart, as the apostle teaches in the words previously read, heeding the order and behest of their masters, waiting on them and following them. In this regard, the prophet makes a comparison in Psalm 123, saying: "As the eyes of servants look to the hands of their masters, as the eyes of a maidservant look to the hands of her mistress, so our eyes look to the Lord our God."

But not only should they diligently carry out their assigned duties when they know someone is watching them. One finds many of these, who appear to be willing to move a mountain as long as someone is watching. But as soon as they are left alone, they begin to lounge around, fold their hands on their chest, then stand up to prattle and carry out useless things, and all the while the work remains mostly undone. These are eye-servants who seek only to please men, working halfheartedly at their assigned tasks. But St. Paul says that they should be obedient to their masters in sincerity of heart, not only before the eyes as if to please men, but from the heart and with goodwill. This is what the centurion in Matthew 8 said about his servants with special approval, and it will be preached about them until the Last Day. He said to the Lord Christ: "I have soldiers[6] under me. If I say to one, 'Go,' he goes, and to another, 'Come here,' he comes, and to my servant, 'Do this,' he does it." Similarly, the wise queen of Sheba praised the servants of Solomon when she saw how all of them, each one in his place, diligently carried out their assigned tasks without any mistakes or complaints. She noted this and praised it as part of the wisdom and the good fortune of King Solomon.

But even though masters and mistresses do not all share the same attitude—indeed, some can occasionally be harsh and angry, nevertheless pious, Christian servants should be no less willing to obey them. For the holy apostle Peter requires this of them when he speaks of their office and writes thus: "Servants, be submissive to your masters with all fear, not only to those who are gentle, but also to those who are harsh," in the same way that children must have patience with their parents when they begin to become harsh; in the same way that subjects must have patience with harsh, strict rulers and must think well of them.

But since masters and mistresses have nothing more valuable and more precious in this life than their children, godly, Christian servants are above all duty-bound, when they are ordered to wait on the children, not to neglect them or lose track of them in any way. Christ testifies to us in the Gospel (Matthew 18) that even the dear, elect angels of God serve the young children. Therefore menservants and maidservants should also not be ashamed to wait on them, and they certainly should not cause

---

6 *Kriegsknecht* – lit. "servants of war"

them to stumble with useless prattle, shameful behavior, speech, words or works. For just as menservants and maidservants can do much good for the children if they themselves are godly people, so they can do great harm to the children of their masters and, with words and deeds, mislead them into all kinds of lavishness, wickedness, and wantonness, if they themselves are evil. But for this they will surely receive the judgment of the Son of God which He pronounced upon all the offenses caused by the world (Mat. 18).

If I may summarize all these things, servants should see to the wellbeing of their masters and mistresses in all things and help to foster what is in their best interest. And they should not disparage their masters in front of other people nor gossip outside of the house about things that might bring trouble upon their masters and mistresses. Also, they must not pilfer or steal anything that has been placed into their hands to manage faithfully, but they should handle it in such a way that their faithfulness and obedience as true Christians is obvious and clearly evident to everyone.

Of course, we cannot fail to mention here that this obedience (as was also shown in previous sermons to be the case with regard to subjects and children) is required only up to a certain point, and extends as far, as wide, and as much as decent and proper things are demanded of them. For God's Word does not call on them or teach them to let themselves be used in dishonest, ungodly, and unreasonable matters. On the contrary, God's Word forbids this in the highest degree, for this is and remains a universal, eternal and unchangeable rule: One must be more obedient to God than to men (Acts 5). Therefore, servants and helpers do wrong who allow themselves to be used for sinful purposes in order to please their masters. Saul's servants did this when, at his command, they led him to a witch. And David's servants did this when they brought to him Bathsheba, Uriah's wife. Absalom's servants also did this when, at his command, they put Amnon to death, contrary to all justice and uprightness. For although Amnon had forfeited his life by raping his sister, it was the place neither of Absalom nor of his servants to put him to death—as little as it was the place of the ten servant boys or armorbearers of Joab to lay hands on Absalom in order to please their master Joab, while bringing the greatest misfortune and heartache to King David (2 Sam. 18). In the same way, the servants of that bloodhound Herod should not have consented to their master in slaughtering the poor little children of Bethlehem.

The servants of King Saul handled the matter much more prudently who would not let themselves be talked into laying hands on the innocent priests (1 Sam. 22). And the officers of the Pharisees also acted wisely, for although they were sent to arrest Christ, they did not carry out such an unjust command (John 7).

Therefore, Christian, godly servants should use discretion and not agree to it when they are ordered to do something improper. Rather, they should fear God, as Joseph did (Gen. 29) when he preferred being thrown into prison rather than acting dishonorably with his master's wife (as she daily, incessantly urged him to do), in spite of the fact that not the least bit of honorable, proper obedience was found lacking in him.

These are the things in which the duty of righteous domestics, menservants and maidservants, consists.

But since human nature is so perverse that it must be driven to what is good, the dear apostle, in the text that was previously read, has offered several reasons by which to motivate all menservants and maidservants to carry out the obedience that has been described. First, he gives them to understand that, when they serve their masters and mistresses, they are actually serving the Lord Christ Himself. This single reason should really make all their work much lighter and more pleasant. For tell me, if Christ still walked on the earth as He did in the past, wouldn't you gladly serve Him, as the two sisters of Lazarus, Martha and Mary, served Him from the bottom of their heart (Luke 10, John 12)? Here you will undoubtedly say: "Yes, of course! Who wouldn't serve Him gladly? For He has redeemed us with His blood and death from sin, death, the devil, hell, and eternal damnation! He, indeed, is worthy, for He earned such great things for us. And besides that, even the angels in heaven are at His service without interruption and carry out all of His commands, as we read in Psalm 103." Well, then! If you feel that way in your heart, then listen to what Paul says to you: When you work diligently for your earthly masters and mistresses, you are performing this service for Christ Himself. And what St. Paul speaks and writes—that was spoken and written from the third heaven, from whence He learned his entire divine doctrine.

Isn't that a powerful reason that should rightly make menservants and maidservants eager to carry out their work faithfully and obediently, knowing that the Lord Jesus Christ counts their work as though it were done to Himself? Thus when a lowly maidservant diligently does her housework, no matter how insignificant it may appear to our reason, she does a far, far better work before God and our Redeemer Jesus Christ than the monks and nuns used to do in the cloisters, who sought to obtain salvation through their work. As it is written concerning such works: "They serve Me in vain with the rules of men" (Mat. 15).

St. Paul does not let the matter rest with this praise by which he has exalted the faithful work of servants. He also holds out to them the reward that they will receive for it. For he says in addition: "Know that whatever good anyone does, he will receive the same from the Lord, whether he is a slave or a free man." With these words he means to teach them that, although they may receive only a small reward on earth for all their hard work and sometimes earn little thanks from men even though they have done the best work possible, nevertheless their reward from our Lord God will not be lost; He will compensate them for it. Of that they should have no doubt. He will compensate them for it both here in time and there in eternity. Paul writes to the Colossians in chapter 3 about the eternal reward laid up in heaven, that they will receive the reward of the inheritance. Not, of course, as if they could purchase and earn the eternal inheritance with God by their service, for Christ alone has earned it for us with His servitude, as it is written in Isaiah 43. Thus there remains no merit on our part, but an inheritance, as St. Paul also calls it "an inheritance." But the dear apostle means to teach with these words that, in view of the fact that the imperishable inheritance has been obtained for them and laid up in heaven for them, they should be all the more eager to do gladly all the work that corresponds to their vocation. And even if they receive little thanks for it here, they should find sincere satisfaction in that they have become heirs of life, by grace, through Christ, and undoubtedly have this inheritance to look forward to. For there in heaven and eternal life they will truly have their reward for the faithful service they did—by grace, as we have just discussed.

Yet God the Lord is also unwilling that they should go unrewarded in this life. For the Lord often raises them up from a lower estate to a better one by way of their obedience, faithfulness, and diligence. According to the Word of the Lord Christ: "He who is faithful in the small matter shall be set over many." The Scriptures have presented us with several servants of this kind, praising their faithfulness. For example, we read about Eleazer, the faithful servant and chief steward of Abraham, how he was earnest and zealous in the business of his master, which he carried out as if he were handling his own possessions. He is still rewarded with praise whenever anyone reads how hard his assigned task was when he went on that errand for his young master, Isaac. He imposed this burden on himself: that he would neither eat nor drink until he obtained Rebecca as a wife for the son of his master. Abraham had already known for some time of his great faithfulness and rewarded him for it, making him the administrator and chief steward over all that God had given him. He even considered making him the heir of all his possessions and goods when he himself still had no son in his old age. Jacob also served his mother's brother Laban for a time and did it with great outward zeal. He could honestly boast that he served him with all his strength, having borne the heat of day and the frost of night, so that no sleep came to his eyes. But even though Laban, as a crass, greedy miser, gave him little thanks for it and didn't give him the pay he had rightly earned but, as Jacob told his wives, changed it and modified his wages ten times, still God gave him his wages by blessing Jacob so that He added to him one sheep after another while daily taking them away from Laban.

Who doesn't know the story of Joseph, who also had to be Potiphar's servant in Egypt? He did his duty with great faithfulness and diligence, and the Lord was with him so that God gave him success in everything he did. And when, by his faithful service, he was exalted and placed as chief steward over all that Potiphar had, the Scripture says that the blessing of the Lord was on all that Potiphar had in his house and in his field. Then, although he was repaid evil by his master and mistress and thrown into prison simply because he would not agree to the indecent lust and desires of his mistress, nevertheless God richly rewarded him for his faithfulness and obedience; He took him who was once a slave and made him a master and prince in all of Egypt. Esther, too, the poor servant girl, was exalted by God and became the wife of the great King Ahasuerus.

In addition to the reasons that have been introduced, the holy, highly enlightened apostle Paul, in his Epistle to Titus, chapter 2, earnestly adds yet another very compelling reason for servants and maidservants and all domestics to consider, and for this reason to be obedient, submissive and faithful. He says: "Command servants to be submissive to their masters, to please them in all (proper) things, not talking back, not embezzling, but showing all good faithfulness, so that they may adorn the doctrine of God our Savior in all things." He reminds them first of their duty to be submissive, faithful, and kind to their masters. Then he adds that it will serve to honor the holy Gospel if the servants who have been converted to Christianity lead such a blameless life in their appointed vocation in the sight of their masters who are still estranged from Christ, that through this godly domestic example their masters may be won for the kingdom of our Lord Jesus Christ.

But he would also point out to them the opposite: that if they are not faithful and submissive, this brings dishonor to God and

His holy Gospel among the unbelieving heathen. He elaborates on this in 1 Timothy 6 with these words: "The servants who are under the yoke should consider their masters worthy of all honor, so that the name and doctrine of God may not be blasphemed." Now, if menservants and maidservants do not wish to bring disrepute on the heavenly doctrine of the divine Word, let them follow the teaching of St. Paul and be obedient to their masters and mistresses. That will bring honor, glory and praise to God and His Word, and it will turn out for their own good as well.

As for unfaithful servants, those who oppose their masters and mistresses oppose God Himself, since they do not obey His commandment. This is what Hagar did in her arrogance, for which her mistress wanted to discipline her. And when she (the maidservant) ran away, she still had to turn back at the behest of the angel and humble herself under her mistress' hand. In addition, if unfaithful servants think that perhaps their masters and mistresses are blind to their unfaithfulness so that it may go on unnoticed, they are really deceiving themselves, because such things do not remain hidden for long, and thus, when they are discovered, it is to the shame of the servants. They give themselves a bad name and leave a shameful memory behind them, departing with a stench, as it happened for Elisha's servant Gehazi. Thus they make themselves hateful to men, and they have God Himself for a Judge who will repay each one as he has deserved, whether he be a servant or a freeman. He will also bring such unfaithful servants and maidservants to ruin and assign them a place with the hypocrites, as the parable of the Lord Christ demonstrates (Luke 12).

But it will go well for the pious, upright servants and maidservants who serve in sincerity of heart, as serving the Lord Jesus Christ. Since they have been faithful in a small thing, they shall, as indicated in God's Word, be placed over many things and shall receive, by grace, the reward of the inheritance. May God—Father, Son, and Holy Spirit—grant this unto us all. Amen.

Ninth Sermon on the Table of Duties:
The Office of Household Masters and Mistresses

Ephesians 6

Masters, do also the same toward them and give up threatening, knowing that your Master is also in heaven, and with Him there is no partiality.

We have before us the third order of the third Christian estate, which consists in the domestic government. In the previous sermon we heard about menservants and maidservants—their vocation, office, work, and daily tasks, that they are obliged to serve their masters who are over them in faithfulness and obedience. Now follows the corollary: how the Holy Spirit has commanded household masters and mistresses to behave toward their household servants.

For masters and mistresses should not imagine that, just because they have been dignified by God in this world with a higher status, they may treat their poor menservants and maidservants however they wish. On the contrary, they are, on both sides, bound by God's Word to one another to a certain extent and in distinct points.

But since St. Paul only deals briefly with this matter, as one whose chief concern here is that masters not be too harsh or unmerciful toward their earthly servants, we will also draw the explanation of this office from other testimonies of the Holy Spirit.

To begin with, since the commandment concerning love for the neighbor extends to all men, therefore masters and mistresses owe their house servants the same general love as men who were also created in God's image and purchased at a high price by Christ, with whom there is neither master nor servant nor any partiality. But even more, one should properly love them as housemates, especially if they are faithful, godly and diligent. As the wise man teaches (Sirach 7): "One should love a godly servant." For through the labor of such servants the whole house will be blessed, as we heard in the previous sermon concerning Joseph. This is also why the patriarch Abraham loved his servant Eleazer, because he was very faithful and godly.

Next, they must strive above all to instruct their servants diligently in God's Word. They themselves (the masters and mistresses) should be like house preachers, explaining to them often and teaching them earnestly the important chief parts in which salvation consists. Otherwise, such young servants go about their business and seldom think too deeply about these important matters. Therefore, masters and mistresses, as those who are more learned, should naturally encourage them in this. Accordingly, after the nobleman in John 4 heard the word of Christ, "Your son lives," and then learned from his servants that his son was healed at that very hour when Jesus had spoken to him, it is written about him that "he believed, with his whole house." Likewise Abraham encouraged his servants to be included by circumcision in God's holy covenant (Gen. 17). So also the godly centurion Cornelius directed and enabled his servants to listen to the word from the mouth of the apostle Peter, even as he did, and they received the gift of the Holy Spirit along with him (Acts 10).

To this end, God ordained the Sabbath Day among His people and commanded them to give menservants and maidservants the opportunity to rest, not only in order to refresh them from their weekly labor, but even more so that they could then hear God's Word and thus have food for their souls.

Furthermore, masters and mistresses ought to set a good example for their servants and domestics in all things, as was also said above about parents. For the example of masters and mistresses has a powerful effect on the domestics, either to drive them to all that is good, or to lead them astray to evil.

And since one has menservants and maidservants on account of housework, and since these days they are not only there to serve, but also to learn something that may be useful to them later when they get home, it befits masters and mistresses faithfully to instruct them in their work and not to withhold any useful information from them. There are surely unfaithful masters out there among craftsmen and others, who only half-teach their apprentices a craft and, out of jealousy, withhold some aspect that they do not wish to reveal. This goes against fairness and Christian love, especially since they are benefiting financially from the service of their apprentices and yet are treating them unfairly.

And since menservants and maidservants in our time are not slaves, as they were in former times, but serve for wages so that they can earn something, it behooves masters and mistresses to give them their full wages at the appointed time—without any complaining—as justice and fairness demand that they should. With regard to the day-laborer, God commanded the people of Israel to give him his wages on the very same day and not to let the sun set on it. "For," says the Lord, "he needs it and sustains his life through it; lest he cry out against you and it become sin to you" (Deu. 24).

But since menservants and maidservants are not usually hired for only a day, but for a certain time agreed upon by both parties, it is right that one should not nefariously withhold their wages from them. For here also, what the Lord announced in the Law about day-laborers is valid, that menservants and maidservants, as poor and needy persons, might sigh to God in their distress and charge you with sin and offense. Therefore, although in former times people were not obliged to pay male and female slaves much for the work they did—the Lord Christ also mentions this in the parable He told (Luke 17) about the servant who, when he has done all that his master commands, still should not expect to receive any thanks from his master—nevertheless God also graciously tempered and softened the Law concerning slaves among His people, so that, if they were let go, they were not to be sent away entirely empty-handed. And whoever wishes in this regard to be stubborn toward male or female servants, withholding their wages from them, let it be said of him, as it is written by the wise man, "Whoever does not give the worker his wages is a bloodhound" (Sirach 35).

But besides the agreed-upon wages, one also owes servants and domestics "fodder and bread," as the Scripture calls it, that is, food and drink, such that they can subsist on it and not have a just cause to complain. There are some masters and mistresses who are quick enough to direct their servants to their work, but then they suddenly become slow and stingy when it comes to providing food and drink, to the point that they measure out only a tiny bit to their servants and practically count the bites that go into their mouths, in such a way that the servants must suffer and endure hunger while they work. This is a miserly sort of frugality. A worker is not only worthy of his wages, but also of his food. Indeed, in the Law it said that one was not allowed to muzzle an ox as it was treading. For this reason, Sirach commanded masters—and Solomon commanded housemothers—how they should behave in this regard. Sirach writes this as a lesson to masters: "To the servant belongs his bread, his punishment, and his work." But the Spirit of God speaks highly of a diligent, godly housemother in Proverbs 31: "She gets up early in the night and gives fodder to her household and food to her maidservants." That is, she gives her maidservants what they need so that they can remain there and continue on. She is frugal, not in such a way that she begrudges them their bread, but in that she gives them their assigned portion of food so that they suffer no want and are thus all the more willing to continue attending to all their work.

Furthermore, it is the duty of Christian, God-fearing masters not to be tyrannical toward their domestics, not ill-tempered, but moderate and kind. St. Paul wanted to place special emphasis on this in his words which we previously read when he spoke of the duty of masters: "Give up threatening," he says. Here the apostle draws from Leviticus 25, where God commanded the Israelites not to rule harshly over those who were sold into servitude from their poverty, but should fear God the Lord, or, as Paul explains this accompanying reason in other words, they should consider that they also have a Master in heaven with whom there is no partiality. "Do not be a lion in your house," says Sirach, "and do not be a tyrant toward your servants." Therefore, they should be afraid before God the Almighty to use any inappropriate force on them or to do anything improper against them out of pride. Instead, they should always bear in mind this striking saying, namely, that they have a Master in heaven who looks kindly upon the needy and the oppressed, hears their prayer, and punishes their oppressors.

On account of this, God also gave His people the law that, if a servant was treated badly by his master, or if it was suspected that he might be treated badly by him or beaten too severely out of wrath and fury—if a servant fled from such a tyrannical master to the authorities, then they were not to return him to his angry master (Deu. 23). In this matter, all masters and mistresses should rightly hold before their eyes the example of the God-fearing and pious man Job, who, although he was more powerful than anyone who lived in the East, did not in any way become puffed up with his power; he was afraid of sinning against the lowliest of his servants, as he himself says: "Have I despised the right of my servant or maidservant when they had a case against me? What will I do when God rises up, and what would I answer when He afflicts? Has not He who made him also made me in the womb? And has He not fashioned a body for him as well as for me?"

Oh, how fervently one could wish that this teaching were taken seriously and taken to heart in a Christian manner! For truly there are many masters and mistresses who think nothing of their menservants and maidservants, who imagine that they cannot possibly sin against them, that our Lord God will not hold them accountable for how they treat them. And so they often behave in an unchristian manner toward them, even when they have done nothing wrong. Experience offers only too many examples of this. We will take some from the Bible. Laban was such a merciless dog. Even though Jacob had served him most diligently, Laban insisted that, if anything of the flock was torn apart by wild animals, Jacob had to answer for it and replace it (Gen. 31). Laban had no thanks to give Jacob, but only grumbled and complained, as Jacob himself complained to him, as he had also complained earlier to his wives. When Joseph, the faithful servant of Potiphar, was accused before him of indecent behavior, Potiphar immediately threw him into prison, without any examination or legitimate investigation. And the Egyptian slave drivers—how mercilessly they beat the Hebrews when Pharaoh forced them to work as slaves, contrary to their former rights and freedom! But God, as a righteous Judge, avenged this pride on all of these unjust tyrants.

We read in particular how things went for the family and descendants of Saul. Because King Saul had put to death the Gibeonites (who had to be servants in Israel), God sent a three-year-long famine upon the land during David's reign. And when David inquired about the reason for the famine, he was told that it had been sent upon Israel by God because of the bloodthirsty house of Saul, since he had killed the Gibeonites. God's wrath could not be appeased except by hanging seven men from the house of Saul, so that the blood of the slaughtered Gibeonites might be avenged and the Lord be reconciled to the land. That is certainly what Paul says here: "Give up threatening, and know that you also have a Master in heaven, with whom there is no partiality."

But none of this means that one should allow menservants and maidservants to be insolent, or shut one's eyes and remain silent whether they do good or evil. For, alongside the kindness we have seen to be required of masters and mistresses toward their servants, the Holy Scriptures also permit at the same time a proper severity, so that the servants are preserved in fear and do not become wanton, lazy and negligent in their work, having been pampered by too much gentleness. We have a fine text concerning this in the 33rd chapter of the Wisdom of Sirach: "To the donkey belong his fodder, his whip, and his burden. To the servant belong his bread, his punishment, and his work. Hold your servant to his work and you will have rest before him. Let him be idle and he will turn into a knight. The yoke and the reins bow the neck; stocks and torment, the evil servant. Hold him to his work, lest he be idle. Idleness teaches great wickedness. Place tasks upon him that befit a servant. If he does not obey, place him in the stocks. But," he says, "do not overly burden him, and maintain moderation in all things."

From this saying of the wise man, it is clear that in all things a strict regimen is to be used with the servants, as Sarah did with her proud maidservant Hagar when she wanted to discipline her. Of course, as has been pointed out, it must be done with proper moderation, lest tyranny be employed under the guise of strictness. What a beautiful letter St. Paul wrote to Philemon concerning his servant Onesimus, who had stolen from his master Philemon and had run away! We read how earnestly Paul pleads with him to take Onesimus back, to be gracious toward him, and to let go of the wrath he was feeling. With these words, he teaches all masters and mistresses that, if their servants are somehow deserving of punishment, even if proper strictness requires that they be punished, still moderation should not be exceeded, and Christian, fraternal love (which we owe to one another in Christ Jesus, whether we are masters or servants) should not be forgotten.

Thus one should also encourage them to work. But, as Sirach says in the words just cited, one should not overly burden them, lest their sighs result in your downfall, as we heard above concerning the Egyptians. In the same way, God's people lamented before God over the Babylonians, saying: "The young had to carry millstones, and the boys stumbled under the load of wood," as Jeremiah wrote in his Lamentations, chapter 5.

When it happens that menservants or maidservants become ill while still in the service of their masters and mistresses, many unchristian masters will let them lie there helpless, like a dumb cow, or even show them the door and drive them out, without ever wondering whether they are lying out on the street or elsewhere, whether they suffer want or not, whether they are dead or alive. They don't care; all they care about is that they are being deprived of their service in the meantime.

But such masters should take care that they do not stir up the wrath of God against themselves with such untimely mercilessness, thus bringing misfortune upon their own homes.

The Lord Christ says in Mat. 7: "All that you would have men do unto you, do that also unto them." Now let your own heart be the judge here: If you were in the place of your sick manservant or maidservant, would you like it if someone let you lie there without any proper help, or if they kicked you out of the house? If you have a respectable attitude, not to mention a Christian conscience, then you will acknowledge that this would be neither godly nor right. Therefore, you can easily conclude that, before God, who is Lord of us all, you have the duty in such a time of need to receive them, properly care for them, and do that which is fitting for those who are not heathens nor Turks nor Tatars, but who are and wish to be known as Christians.

Consider the example of the centurion in Capernaum (Mat. 8), how deeply invested he was in his sick servant's wellbeing, how earnestly he prayed to the Lord Christ for him and prayed through others that Christ would help him—no different than a father who concerns himself about his child. So the centurion did for his servant. This is explained every year in the Sunday Gospel as an example for all Christian masters and mistresses.

On the other hand, the Holy Spirit sets before us a fine story in 1 Samuel 30, demonstrating how God repays the mercilessness of masters toward their sick servants. For the Amalekites, in David's absence, had set fire to the town of Ziklag (which David had obtained as a dwelling for himself and his own from King Achish) and took away everything they found, including women and children (who belonged to David and his men). When David returned and learned of this, it just so happened that he found a servant lying on the road whose master had abandoned him, since he had become sick. He then learned from this servant about the situation, where he could overtake the Amalekites and attack them. So it was that the Amalekites were defeated, and among them the unfriendly master, who had abandoned his servant on account of his weakness, was struck down as well, and through his servant's direction, he received the wages of his merciless harshness.

Thus Christians will also, in this area, omit nothing for the care of their domestics, menservants and maidservants. Instead, they will do what God has ordained so that their servants do not lack anything in the way of assistance and help, or suffer on account of the weakness of their flesh—which they themselves would also gladly be rid of.

In conclusion, it is right and required alike by natural law and by God's Word that, as much as possible, you protect your menservants and maidservants against the improper threats of others and that you see to it that they get justice by legitimate means and measures. For, since you are their master, they naturally have recourse to you in such a case; they have the right and the power to call on you, as their appointed master, for help, so that you come to their aid for the sake of justice, in order that they may not be unjustly injured by others. The 33rd chapter of the wise man Sirach expressly mentions this matter, where we read: "If you have a servant, think of him as you think of yourself. For whoever does something against him is seeking your life and limb." That is as much as to say: Your servant must otherwise stand by your side in danger, and, if necessary, risk life and limb for you so that no unseemly harm be done to you by others. Therefore, it is surely right that you should also think about him, especially because the very one who takes aim at your servant is also likewise taking aim at you as his master. He desires to destroy your servant so that he can then set himself more securely against you, his master.

Thus, in this sermon, masters and mistresses are reminded of their duty toward their domestics, workers, menservants and maidservants—what they ought to do for them and how they are to act and behave toward them, according to God and His Word and also for the sake of justice and fairness. May the Almighty God cause them to consider this in godly fear, and may He grant every Christian in particular to recognize his legitimate vocation in which the Lord has placed him and to adorn it with due obedience, so that we may all be found to be faithful menservants and maidservants in the great household of God the heavenly House-father, and one day in heaven, become masters through Christ. May God help us all to that end! Amen.

Tenth Sermon on the Table of Duties: Young People in General

1 Peter 5

Young people, be submissive to the elderly and show humility in this. For God opposes the proud, but gives grace to the humble. So humble yourselves now under the mighty hand of God, that He may exalt you in His time.

Beloved in the Lord Christ, just as each the estate in the Christian Table of Duties has its text and lesson, as we have heard and noted thus far, so also do young people in general have their own lesson and reminder therein. For since it generally holds true with young people that, if they are not continually maintained in Christian discipline, they can easily go astray on account of their lack of understanding—for children and youth are conceited, and "he who is not tried understands little," as the saying goes—therefore it is useful and good, and also necessary, that a special chapter concerning the youth be placed in the Table of Duties. With the intervention of divine grace, we will now explain this in a simple manner from the words that were just read, which have been taken from the fifth chapter of St. Peter's First Epistle, where the dear apostle speaks to the youth in this way: "Young people, be submissive to the elderly and show humility in this." This is an apostolic—indeed, even more, a divine—commandment which can by no means be despised. For we should not view what St. Peter teaches here as the word of men. It is the Holy Spirit who compelled and inspired this to be written and who commanded it to be presented to the poor, uninformed youth.

Therefore, the Spirit of God reminds young people of this virtue that is especially important for them. For it often happens that the wretched Satan afflicts them almost more than other people with regard to pride, conceit, and arrogance, so that they presumptuously think too highly of themselves when they find that they are adorned with fine gifts of body and demeanor.

In order to confront this, they should always have before their eyes this, their lesson from St. Peter in the lection that was just read. It shows them that they should break this inborn pride through the power of the Holy Spirit and not desire to surpass the elderly. Rather, they should be all the more submissive to them in proper, genuine, unfeigned Christian humility and lowliness of heart. God the Lord also included this in His holy Law when He commanded in Leviticus 19: "Before a gray head you shall rise, and you shall honor the elderly." He then lays the foundation and gives the reason: "For you shall fear your God." With these words, He wishes to demonstrate that whoever honors the elderly shows thereby his fear of God. But whoever does not hold them in honor shows thereby that he does not fear God, or else he would duly follow and obey this commandment of His.

But St. Peter wished to solidify his reminder with accompanying reasons: "God opposes the proud," he says, "but gives grace to the humble." It pleases God when a young man humbles himself before the elderly, and it also pleases men. It brings him favor and grace with the people, so that they praise him and say: "That must surely be an upright young man, who knows how to behave toward elderly people and toward everyone else, with all discipline and deference." This says a lot before men.

Accordingly, God also gives grace to the humble, so that He increases His divine gifts and grace in such a humble, young, disciplined heart, as He demonstrated in Joseph, the godly young man in Egypt, and in Daniel and his companions Shadrach, Meshach and Abednego. They behaved in all lowliness of spirit toward God and toward men, with humility and deference. Therefore God increased His gifts in them and exalted them, making Joseph a master over all Egypt (Gen. 41, Dan. 2), making Daniel and his companions officials of the great Babylonian monarch and empire. Thus it is not in vain that Peter says: "Humble yourselves under the mighty hand of God, so that He may exalt you in His time."

Young people should not become haughty if they have received gifts, nor should they wish to be seen as more important than the older adults because of them. One can surely find young, foolish people from time to time in all kinds of estates, crafts and trades who think they are much wiser and more skillful than the older adults. Therefore they are unable to keep their supposedly great skill to themselves, but burst forth with it as in a premature birth. It goes for them as it went for the young Elihu in the Book of Job, chapter 32. Even though he must have recognized that it would be right to let the older men speak while the younger men kept quiet, still, since he thought he knew how to confront Job far better and more reasonably than Job's older friends had done, he could no longer contain himself. He spoke up and glorified himself, boasting about how full of wisdom he was so that the spirit in his body was compelling him. In the same way, there are some who think they are smarter and better educated than those who are older. They think that whatever an older person has made cannot possibly be made well; the youth can do it better. They can, as they say, "correct the Magnificat." They think their belly would burst if they had to keep quiet about their skill. It goes for them as Sirach says in chapter 19: "A fool bursts forth like a premature child who wants to get out. When a word is stuck in a fool, it is like an arrow stuck in a hoof." In other words, the foolhardiness of the young and inexperienced is described with words and pictures in such a way that they should become averse to such insolence.

Now, if you are young and the evil foe tries to instill such haughty thoughts in you, saying to you: "Look! You can do something, too. You must step forward and let yourself be seen and heard. The older people can't do everything. They're becoming senile!," then you should remember this text from the Table of Duties. "Young people, be submissive to the old and show humility in this." You should remember that it is written: "Do not think yourself smarter than the old, for they also learned it from their fathers. You can learn from them what you should answer, when necessary." Be aware of the teaching that the same wise man offers in chapter 32: "The elder should speak, for it is fitting for him, as one who is experienced." And again: "A young person may indeed also speak once or twice, if he must and if he is asked. He should keep his remarks brief and control himself, as one who knows little and prefers to remain silent. He should not consider himself equal with the masters, and when an elder speaks, the young man should not prattle on."

So you should always give preference to those who are older. This humility is not to your detriment, but to your honor, for "as the thunder brings great lightning, so shame brings with it great favor," as Sirach again gives us an account of this in chapter 32. Nor is this humility to your shame; it is required before God. And why would the youth be ashamed to honor their elders and give them preference, when indeed old age is an honorable thing in and of itself, and we all desire to grow old? As Sirach writes in chapter 8, the elderly have certainly experienced more, seen more and heard more, and therefore know better how to discuss things and to draw one conclusion after another. Therefore the Scripture again reminds and admonishes: "Do not despise the speech of the wise, but conform to their sayings, for you can learn something from them, including how you should restrain yourself in the presence of great men." Indeed, from the story of King Rehoboam we learn that there is greater counsel, understanding, wisdom, and experience among the elderly than among those who have not yet reached many years, who have not yet been able to see or hear very much. The older men gave him a very good and salutary counsel, that, in order to appease the ten tribes of Israel, he should lessen their burden. But the young, inexperienced men gave him the opposite counsel, and their counsel was so bad that it caused those ten tribes in Israel to break away from the house of David on a single day.

All of this is to say that the young should be submissive to those who are older. But whoever refuses to do this and instead despises old age shall, in turn, be despised and shall fail to reach old age. So it happened with the impertinent youth, the wicked, spoiled brats at Bethel who mocked the old prophet Elisha, calling him "baldy." They were not counted worthy to grow a single day older or to live a single day longer. For two bears came out of the woods and tore them apart as punishment for having despised the old age of the holy man of God.

This is what the text of St. Peter is talking about. But since this text does not address the entire life of the youth, but only one aspect of it—although it certainly deals with a very important virtue of the youth, namely, Christian humility—we will explain a bit more from the Scriptures this theme of young people in general, so that thereby people can picture for themselves how their whole life should be ordered so that they may be found well-pleasing to God and to men.

First of all, they should consider early in their tender, young years how they will obtain a right, honorably old age, which is a matter of wisdom and true godliness. True old age is a matter of honor, not of living a long life or attaining to many years. Wisdom among men is the real gray hair, and a spotless life is the true old age, as we read in the Book of Wisdom, chapter 4. To this belongs a right knowledge of God, as John admonishes the Christian youth in his First Epistle, chapter 2: "I write to you, children, for you know the Father." This knowledge they gain from God's Word and from their holy Catechism, through which—if they daily apply themselves to it as a spiritual exercise, if they grow and progress in it—they will also go from budding youth to full-grown adulthood and "a perfect man, who is in the measure of Christ," of which Paul writes in Ephesians 4, namely, that they "attain to the knowledge of the Son of God, of the full adulthood of Christ, and no longer be children who are moved here and there by every wind of doctrine through the deceit of men."

To this also pertains true fear of God, which is likewise explained from God's Word. When young people pay attention to what God requires of them and to what He also offers them, then they are careful to lead a spotless life before the Lord, as we are told again in Psalm 119 where the prophet says: "How shall a young person keep his way blameless? By holding to Your words."

In order that they may walk blamelessly in this blessed and holy way of God's commandments and not stray from it onto the path of the world, they should gladly be involved in those things by which they may learn the true, heavenly wisdom, of which the fear of the Lord is a fountainhead and beginning, that is, they should associate with older people who are pious and godly, who find joy and delight in speaking about God and His Word. This edifies the youth, and through it they progress in the blessed school of heavenly, divine wisdom. Solomon gives them this same faithful counsel in his Proverbs, chapter 13: "He who walks with the wise man becomes wise," says he. And Sirach says in chapter 6: "Associate gladly with the elderly, and where a wise man is, abide with him. Hear the Word of God gladly, and note the good sayings of wisdom. When you see a man with understanding, go to him quickly, and go in and out with him continually. Always consider God's command, and meditate continually on His Word. He will make your heart perfect and give you wisdom, as you desire."

But just as the company of wise and learned people is edifying for the tender youth, so also the young should avoid and flee from the company of the wicked, if they want to be delivered from all the deception and mischief that spring from such company. For it is not in vain that the Holy Spirit has so earnestly warned us about this. "Do not be deceived. Evil company corrupts good habits," says Paul (1 Cor. 15). "He who touches pitch will sully himself with it. And he who associates with a proud man will learn pride," says Sirach in chapter 13. "For bad examples lead astray and corrupt the good in a person, and alluring desire twists innocent hearts," says Solomon in the Book of Wisdom, chapter 4. And "he who is the companion of fools will experience misfortune," as it is written in Proverbs 13.

Therefore, if you are a young man and you see someone who likes to curse, who doesn't like to go to church to hear the sermon, who is disobedient to father and mother, quarrelsome and undisciplined, who is a scoundrel in words and actions or in other ways, flee from him as from the wretched devil himself, for he is the devil's ambassador. Where the devil himself cannot enter, he sends such people in through whom he advances his work. Beware of them and follow the teaching of Solomon when he says: "My child, if the wicked sinners entice you, do not follow" (Proverbs 1).

And since young people are, by nature, more inclined to merriment than those who are older, it will be very important for them to guard themselves in this matter. For Satan is quick to take advantage of this in order to seduce the foolish, unthinking young men into the lust of this world, so that they begin to be secure, wild, crude, and godless. They waltz into all kinds of sin and shame while they forget about discipline and the fear of the Almighty, thinking to themselves, "Why would you want to expend your energy on those things—how to be godly? That will come by itself when you're older. Then you will straighten yourself out and get on the path. Until then, you have to take advantage of the world so that you won't have wasted your time here." They are thus urged into the way of sinners and mockers who rush securely to their own destruction, who speak like those about whom we read in the Book of Wisdom, chapter 2: "Come, now! Let us live well, while we have the chance. Let us use our body while it's still young. We want to fill ourselves with the best wine and ointments. Let us not miss out on the May flowers! Let us wear garlands made of fresh roses, before they fade. Let none of us want for fancy attire, so that, no matter what, all men may know that we were merry. Indeed, there is nothing more to life than that. Let us not give a thought to the poor righteous men who are oppressed, nor to the widows, nor to the old men. Let us not worry about the correction of the old gray heads. Whatever we can do, we should do, for he who cannot do as he pleases is worth nothing." But what does the wise man say to this in the same chapter? He says: "They make these plans, and they fail. Their wickedness has blinded them so that they do not acknowledge God's hidden judgment, for they have no hope that a holy life will be rewarded, and they pay no attention to the honor that will be afforded to blameless souls."

Yes, indeed, it happens to many young people that, while they had hoped to take advantage of the world and its pleasures for awhile longer, they are suddenly taken away by temporal death and must appear before the judgment seat of God sooner than they had expected. A man may be young and strong now, but in an instant he is cut down and powerless. And since he is not found in the fear of God, he goes, body and soul, to his temporal and eternal ruin. For "all flesh is like grass, and all their glory is like the flowers of the field. The grass withers, the flowers fade, for the Spirit of the Lord blows on them" (Isa. 46). Therefore, do not grow conceited because of your youth. You are neither too handsome nor too young for our Lord God to find you, and that, when you least expect it.

But "remember your Creator in your younger years," as Solomon teaches in Ecclesiastes 12, and keep Him before your eyes. Allow yourself to be led and disciplined by God's Word. Bind it on your hand as a sign, and, as Moses says, "write it on your doors as a remembrance before your eyes." In this way, you will guard your soul unblemished by a sinful life. Joseph is a notable example of this. Although he was young, nevertheless the fear of God was in his heart like an iron wall, so that Satan was unable to overpower him or compel him to do wrong when he was urged to unchastity by his master's wife. Indeed, that is also the spiritual victory against Satan, against the world and its perverse pleasures. The holy Evangelist John praises this victory and triumph to Christian young people with these words: "I have written to you, young ones, because you are strong, and the Word of God abides with you, and you have conquered the evil one."

But here someone will say: "Are young people, then, to have no pleasure or enjoyment whatsoever? Must they lead a Carthusian life? Does not their youth itself induce them to happiness rather than gloominess?" Here we will let the preacher Solomon answer, who gives this response to such a question: "Rejoice, O young one, in your youth, and let your heart be of good cheer in your youth. Do whatever your heart desires and your eyes find pleasant (understand—in honorable things), and **know that for all of this God will bring you into judgment.**" That is as much as to say: When you are surrounded by pleasures, you may indeed enjoy yourself; God certainly allows you this. But keep His fear and His judgment ever hovering before your eyes, so that, when you are tempted by bad company or by your own corrupt flesh to excess, to indulge too much in such pleasures, you may then restrain yourself and allow yourself to be ruled by the fear of the Almighty God, and consider that God will one day bring you before His judgment seat for all the things you have done and will require that you answer for it, as the Son of God says in Matthew 12. "Men must give an account for every careless word they have spoken." This fear of the Lord and blessed consideration of His eternal judgment will keep you in check, so that even in the midst of pleasures you keep your way pure before God, lest with revelry, drinking and drunkenness, pride and glory, filthy words or works, you sin against God your Creator and against His holy Majesty.

Those young men who have thus preserved themselves in the things they were to do and leave undone, as we have heard—they are the ones who have now obtained an honorable old age that consists in the blessed knowledge of God and in a spotless life. They have obtained the dearest victory of all: the victory against Satan. Then their youth is in no way to be despised, as St. Paul writes about his young disciple Timothy, for they now walk their path purely and blamelessly. They are acceptable to God and acclaimed among men, as it is written: "A young man through wisdom is glorified among the people and honored among the elders." Such young people rise up beneficially to take the place of the older ones who are fading away, so that they serve both God and men with great praise and benefit in the spiritual and secular realms. "They obtain here on earth an immortal name, and leave an eternal memorial with those who come after them" (Wisdom of Solomon 8).

In this way, young Christian people store up for themselves a good treasure for their future old age, namely, true blessedness. For if they have been diligent in these things in their youth, they carry with them a good and quiet conscience into their old age, which is better than all the things for which the world yearns, with which they can also ameliorate all the sorrow, sickness, and trouble that come with old age, because they know that they have a gracious God in heaven, so they await with joy the dissolution of their body. On the other hand, those who destroy their precious youth and misuse it with sins and vices—they carry with them into old age a gnawing, consuming worm, namely, a bad and restless conscience, which tortures them more severely than all that could possibly happen to them in the flesh.

May the almighty God and Father of our Lord Jesus Christ, through His Holy Spirit, graciously grant to the poor, tender, inexperienced youth to consider all this at all times, and to direct their life accordingly, so that they may ever grow and advance in the heavenly wisdom that consists in true knowledge of God, genuine fear of God and irreproachable conduct, that they may not disrupt the blessed work begun in them in Holy Baptism, but be preserved until the end and perfected. May God—Father, Son and Holy Spirit, worthily praised forever and ever—grant this to them and to us all. Amen.

Eleventh Sermon on the Table of Duties: Widows

1 Timothy 5

She is a true widow who is alone, who puts her hope in God and continues day and night in prayer and supplication. But she who lives in pleasure is dead while living.

In the Table of Duties, beloved in the Lord, the widows also have their special lesson placed before them from God's Word, which we have just heard read from St. Paul. And since such persons have need both of comfort and of instruction, we will first discuss the comfort given them by the testimonies of the Holy Spirit—where they stand with God, what their hope and confidence in their bereaved estate as widows should be. Second, how their conduct, life, doing, and leaving undone should be ordered so that they may be pleasing to God and heaven and to pious, God-fearing men on earth.

THE FIRST PART: Their Comfort

To begin with, if widows want to know how God is minded toward them, they must not allow themselves to be led astray by the world's judgment. For the children of the world commonly act, with words and deeds, as if it were impossible to sin against the poor widows. So the widows are often not only despised, but must also suffer injustice. And if they are not firmly supported with the comfort of God's Word, they become demoralized because of it as they consider how they are spurned by men. Thus they may also consider themselves to be all the more disregarded by God because of their bereaved estate.

Therefore they should rely on the Scriptures to know how God is minded toward them, for God's thoughts are not men's thoughts. That is, God does not love a person because he is rich, powerful, highly respected, admirable, and worthy, while disregarding the poor and abandoned. On the contrary, God takes more pleasure in that which is poor, needy, weak, disrespected, and despised by the world, so that He may put to shame what is otherwise respectable, powerful, rich, and noble, as St. Paul teaches in his First Epistle to the Corinthians. In the same way also the king and prophet says and sings with wonder in the 113th Psalm: "Where is there a God like the Lord our God, who is seated on high and yet looks upon the lowly in heaven and on earth?" But most of all and above all else, He turns toward those who have a contrite spirit, as it is written in Psalm 34. "The Lord is near to those whose heart is broken, and helps those whose spirit is contrite." Isaiah likewise speaks of God and testifies in chapter 57 of his prophecy: "Indeed, He dwells on high and in the holy place, but also with those who have a contrite and humble spirit, that He may revive the spirit of the humble and comfort the heart of the contrite." Therefore the Lord Christ also praises as blessed those who mourn and are poor in spirit in this world, for they shall be gladdened (Luke 6).

And just as God looks upon all poor, sorrowful, forsaken persons in general with His divine grace and favor, so also He especially looks upon the widows. For in Psalm 68 He calls Himself a "Father of the fatherless and a Defender of the widows." In a similar way, God has also, as it were, placed a hedge and a wall around them in the Law by means of a solemn commandment, that no one should improperly afflict or grieve them (Exodus 22). "You shall not afflict any widow or fatherless child, lest they cry out to me and I hear their cry. Then My wrath will be aroused so that I put you to death with the sword, and your wives will become widows, and your children will become fatherless."

The Lord stresses this powerfully in the Scriptures, for with great earnestness He commends the widows to the secular authorities—to all rulers and judges—that they should grant them shelter and protection against all the unjust power of their adversaries. For this is what the Lord says about them through the prophet Isaiah: "Help the downtrodden. Give justice to the fatherless. And plead the case of the widows. So come, then, and let us reason together. Though your sin is blood-red, it shall become snow-white. And though it is like the color of roses, it shall become like wool." The highly enlightened teacher Sirach writes similarly in chapter 4: "Deliver him who suffers wrong from him who treats him unjustly, and be unafraid when you must judge. Be as a father to the fatherless and as a housemaster to their mothers (the widows). Then you will be like a son of the Most High, and He will love you more than your mother does."

On the other hand, God the Lord has threatened severe punishment—indeed, even the desolation of the country—if unjust power is exerted against the widows, or if justice is not rendered to them in their cases before the court. In the first chapter of Isaiah, God charges the great princes of the kingdom of Judah with this and threatens His wrath against them, along with their downfall, because they did not esteem the widows and the fatherless in the courts. "Your princes are renegades," He says, "and the companions of thieves. They all gladly accept a bribe and seek after gifts. They refuse justice to the fatherless, and the widow's case does not come before them." In Zechariah 7 the Lord says: "Judge uprightly and let each one show kindness and mercy to his brother. And do not deal unjustly with the widows, fatherless, foreigners, and poor, and let no one plot any evil against his brother in his heart. But they wouldn't listen, and they turned their backs to Me and plugged their ears so that they wouldn't hear." He then adds shortly thereafter: "It is for this reason that such great wrath has come from the Lord of Sabaoth and has gone out just as it was preached." And Sirach 35: "The Lord helps the poor and shows no partiality; He listens to the prayer of the afflicted and does not despise the prayer of the fatherless or the widow when they complain. The tears of the widows may well run down her cheeks, but they cry out against the one who causes them to flow."

Thus God has also proven His fatherly, gracious concern for the poor widows with clear examples from the holy, divine Scriptures, as demonstrated in the story of Ruth. As a widow, she behaved well in every way toward her mother-in-law, and God deemed her worthy before anyone else at that time of becoming a grandmother of the Son of God. And although she was a foreigner, she came into the genealogy of our Lord and Messiah.

In the same way, we read about the widow of Zarephath (1 Kings 17), how God took fatherly care of her during the time of famine, so that, according to the promise made through the prophet Elijah, her oil jar did not run dry nor did her flour supply run out until the day when God again chose to give rain on the earth. And to the widow whose husband had been among the sons of the prophets (who cried out to the prophet Elisha on account of her creditors who were demanding payment from her), God, through a special miracle, granted so much oil that she not only had enough to pay her debts, but had enough left over that she could continue to provide for herself and her sons.

Yes, how tenderly our Lord Christ Himself received the sorrowful widow (Luke 7) whose son had died and was being carried out for burial! He spoke to her favorably and comforted her with words and deeds. He raised up her dead son and thus demonstrated in this glorious, unheard-of deed that such grieving persons are dear to His heart.

From all these examples, Christian widows can conclude that their estate is not at all disregarded by God, but that, on the contrary, the persons in this estate are beloved, precious, and acceptable to Him. Therefore they must comfort themselves with this in their pain and sorrow, not only against the world's hatred and unjust power, but also against the ideas and thoughts by which they might otherwise become dejected, as if God didn't care at all about them. Against such notions they must now discern the Holy Spirit's opinion from the infallible Word of God: God cares for them. He has His face turned toward them and never, ever wishes to abandon them in their grief. So much for the first part of the sermon.

THE SECOND PART: Their Conduct

We must now take up, in the second place, the matter of how widows are to conduct themselves in their behavior, life and demeanor. For it is surely a glorious promise and an exceedingly great comfort that we have hitherto noted concerning the widows. But we also hear that St. Paul very appropriately distinguishes between different kinds of widows, speaking of some who are dead while living, because they live in all kinds of pleasure-seeking, and therefore must not in any way appropriate this comfort to themselves. More will be said of these widows shortly. How should those widows conduct themselves who are rightly counted among true Christians and who rightly share in the aforementioned comfort? Here St. Paul again makes a distinction between young and old widows. Concerning young widows, he says that they should marry (understand—if they cannot keep themselves pure outside of the marital estate). Likewise, that they should raise and manage their children, that is, they should properly see to their household management so that their children are cared for and their husbands have no complaint.

So it is that Ruth, since she was still a young widow, did well and right when she remarried, raised children, and in this second marriage gave birth to Obed, from whom Christ was descended according to the flesh, as revealed in the genealogy of the Lord Christ (Mat. 1).

For some of the ancient teachers of the Church erred when they held the opinion that remarriage is forbidden to Christians and is comparable to adultery, as is demonstrated in this and many other passages. We have here the clear text of St. Paul, who expressly permitted remarriage to widows. Indeed, he actually desires that widows should seek a second marriage in the name of God, remarry, raise children, and devote themselves to managing a home rather than bring shame to the Gospel through an unchaste life. The apostle also confirms this in his Epistles to the Romans and to the Corinthians. In Romans 7 he says: "A woman is subject to her husband. As long as her husband lives, she is bound to the law. But if her husband dies, she is free from the law of the husband. If she is with another man while her husband lives, she is called an adulteress. But if her husband dies, she is free from the law, so that she is not an adulteress if she is with another man." And in 1 Corinthians 7 it is written: "To the unmarried and the widows I say: It is good for them if they also remain as I am (understand—on account of the present necessity at that time, as St. Paul himself explains). But if they cannot restrain themselves, then let them marry; it is better to marry than to burn." And again: "A wife is bound to the law as long as her husband lives. But if her husband falls asleep, she is free to marry whomever she wants, as long as it is done in the Lord."

Thus these young widows, as long as they remain widows, must conduct themselves in all discipline and chastity. But in the second marriage that follows (into which they enter), they should in all things behave as we have already discussed in the corresponding part of the explanation of the Table of Duties concerning wives.

As pertains to the older widows—the ones who have now reached an age at which they cannot otherwise readily become engaged, the Holy Spirit prescribes to them, through St. Paul, some regulations according to which they should order and live out the remainder of their life. With regard to those who have children or immediate family, they should instruct them in managing the home, in work and in all discipline and decency, so that they learn how to properly provide for their home and not be allowed to forget to repay their parents, "for this is good and pleasing to God," says the apostle. In this way, the godly widow Naomi instructed her daughter-in-law Ruth in good things of this kind (Ruth 3), so that she obtained exceedingly great status and has been praised by small and great as being a virtuous wife.

St. Paul then requires of them that they "wash the feet of the saints," that is, that they show abject kindness to godly Christians—especially to foreigners—for the sake of the Gospel.

Wealthy widows of our day can and should also do this, according to the circumstances of their provisions. But poor widows who themselves depend on the help and charity of others can also do this in a certain way and to a certain extent, namely, by waiting on the sick in their needs, by nursing them in their weakness. For one depends on such people in a time of need. They should also willingly allow themselves to be used for this. That is also called "washing the feet of the saints." God considers it an acceptable work. Besides, He has commanded us to serve the sick and has promised that rich rewards will accompany such service.

In addition to this, Paul has also described in the words previously read other virtues of a godly widow. For example, she is "alone." That is, she is not one to always be going out, running around town, but stays quietly at home, except for when she is called out to wait on sick or disabled people.

Another virtue described by the apostle: "They should put their hope in God." For although it is also proper for other Christians to hope in the living God, widows have more reason to withdraw from all that is temporal and to focus their hope only and alone upon God the Lord in heaven, since they are otherwise abandoned in the world and the wicked often cause them grief. All sorts of adversity accompanies them in their forsaken, bereaved estate, which is all the more reason why they should put all their hope, trust, and confidence in God, as the One who can and will be for them a refuge, shelter, and defense in all their sorrow. In order to strengthen this hope in God, widows must remember all that was pointed out in the first part of this sermon, namely, how comforting it is that God calls Himself their Father, Defender, and Redeemer, who will care for them with special grace, vindicate their just cause against the oppression of the children of the world, and appear to them with grace and help in every need.

Next, the holy apostle requires that they should "continue day and night in prayer." This should be their spiritual exercise, that they should continually be found going to church, hearing

God's Word, using the holy Sacraments, and steadfast in holy prayer, not only for themselves, but for all men, especially for holy Christendom, that God would guard her against all her foes—against Satan and all the gates of hell. For since widows are pleasing to God, their prayer does not go up in vain, as the wise man Sirach testifies in chapter 35. And since they have practically died with regard to the temporal things of the world, they should certainly trouble themselves with God and pray without ceasing that He would guard His Holy Christian Church, together with her ministers and members, in the blessed knowledge of His almighty, saving Word and in holy, inoffensive conduct; that He would send workers into His spiritual harvest, and also give His Holy Spirit and divine power to the Word, that the kingdom of our dear Lord and Savior Jesus Christ may be advanced among men and many people ripped out of the devil's clutches and brought to the fellowship of eternal life.

We have a living example of such a respectable, God-fearing widow in the prophetess Anna (Luke 2), whom the Evangelist praises for being alone, for having her hope placed in God, for never leaving the temple, and for serving God day and night with fasting and prayer.

Now that is something precious before God and praiseworthy before godly men. It is pleasing to God and edifying to His holy Church when they ever devote themselves with their prayers to the prosperity and to the blessed and unhindered progress of the dear Christian Church on earth. In this way, through these spiritual exercises they can make their sorrowful estate lighter for themselves, knowing that, after this passing, toilsome life, they have an eternal life in Christ the Lord to look forward to.

But since there are different kinds of widows, and there are many who are not alone but like to go out, who do not place their hope in God and do not trouble themselves at all with prayer, the apostle has not been negligent also in having their own chapter read to them. He says of them: "But the widow who lives in pleasure is dead while alive." That is as much as to say: If a widow begins to devote herself to worldly pleasure, to become mired in sin and shame; if she thinks that, now that she is free from her deceased husband, she can do no wrong and so is free to wallow in the filth of this world and do whatever she wants, then she has thereby stubbornly removed herself from the gracious protection of the Almighty and from all His grace. And even though she may think that she is alive and doing just fine when she gives free rein to the flesh, she is actually dead before God, because she is cut off from the blessed fellowship of God, who alone is and gives life. Thus she is deprived of the future eternal life.

But what could ever be more foolish than for a person to put his eternal welfare in jeopardy for the sake of temporal, momentary pleasure—or worse, displeasure!—and quite intentionally to rush into the unquenchable flames of hellfire?

Therefore, widows must not despise this thunderbolt of the Law. It is aimed at their soul, where they are devoted to the world and to worldly pleasures. For they hear that, just as God-fearing widows have a comforting promise and assurance, so also a terrible punishment lies in store for those who either live in unchastity or otherwise behave without propriety. For surely there are many who do nothing except for run around town, spreading new tales here and there, causing all kinds of trouble, quarreling, and arguments among the people. They entice young workers into their houses, telling them, "It's all right. It doesn't matter." Then they arrange a relationship between them, from which often grow the most burdensome dealings, which have their beginning from this wicked match-making, instigated by the devil. True Christian widows will guard themselves from all this and will follow the apostolic admonition of St. Paul.

Thus far concerning widows. May the merciful and compassionate God grant to all widows His grace, and the power and attendance of His good and Holy Spirit. May He comfort them in their sorrow, instill in their hearts a steadfast hope in God, and move them to be fervent in prayer and in respectable, holy conduct, so that they may have, here in time, a living comfort in God the Lord, and, there in eternity, all fullness and satisfaction. May God—Father, Son, and Holy Spirit—give and grant this unto them and unto us all. Amen.

Twelfth and Final Sermon on the Table of Duties: What Is Owed to All Men in Common

Romans 13

Do not owe anyone anything, except that you love one another, for whoever loves the other has fulfilled the Law. For when it says, "You shall not commit adultery," "You shall not murder," "You shall not steal," "You shall not give false testimony," "You shall not covet anything," and if there is any other commandment, it is summed up in this saying: "You shall love your neighbor as yourself."

Thus far we have heard from the Christian Table of Duties about all kinds of estates and how Christians are to conduct themselves in them—church ministers and hearers, rulers and subjects, husbands and wives, parents and children, masters and menservants, mistresses and maidservants, as well as the youth in general and widows.

Now, with this sermon, we wish to conclude the explanation of the Table of Duties. It still remains to discuss what everyone owes to all men in common. Paul teaches us this very simply in the words that have just been read.

Let us hear and diligently consider these things together (since they apply to all men together). St. Paul says this: "Do not owe anyone anything, except that you love one another." That is, this should be your common debt that you pay to one another, which can thus never be entirely retired. You never cease owing this debt to show genuine, true, unfeigned love toward one another in word and deed, thereby serving one another from the heart. St. Paul offers some reasons as the basis for this brief teaching: "For whoever loves the other has fulfilled the Law." This is not to be understood as if anyone could keep God's Law perfectly in this world, for this is simply impossible for us men due to the outward corruption of our nature. For the Law demands of us a completely pure nature; a pure heart; pure, holy thoughts, words, and deeds; and thus the most perfect obedience. But we are conceived and born in sin. We are, by nature, children of wrath, just as the others, so that no man can say, "My heart is pure." For how could a man born of woman be pure when he is wretched and loathsome and laps up iniquity like water, whose very imaginations and thoughts are evil from childhood on? Indeed, the whole world's mouth is stopped so that no one can satisfy or fulfill God's Law, because it is weakened by our corrupt flesh, as Paul teaches in Romans 8.

Then how must the apostle's words be understood, when they expressly say, "Whoever loves the other has fulfilled the Law"? Answer: The Scripture speaks of the Law of love in two ways. First, as it was given by God through Moses, which, as noted, demands perfect obedience on the part of man. Then, the Scripture speaks of the Law and commandment of love as Christ renewed it in the New Testament. He has not laid upon us the unbearable burden of the Law, which He took upon Himself, having fulfilled the entire Law. Rather, it is satisfied with the beginning of obedience, which is still true obedience, when a person loves his neighbor from the heart, even though it is done in imperfection.

Because of this twofold consideration, the commandment concerning love is called both an old and also a new commandment (1 John 2): old, because, in short, in its strict sense, it demands a thoroughly perfect man; but new, because the Son of God has softened it, and because He has given the command to His believers, now that He has taken upon Himself the unbearable load. Although our new obedience is imperfect, He wishes to be content with it. To this end He also gives His Holy Spirit, that we may serve Him, not under compulsion, but willingly; not in the old way of the letter, but in the new way of the Spirit. Therefore John also writes about the commandment of Christ (as He has laid it upon us): "His commandments are not difficult." And St. Paul says that this commandment concerning love is not impossible for us, to the extent that Christ has softened it, when he writes to the Galatians in chapter 6: "Let each one carry the burden of the other. In this way you will fulfill the law of Christ."

From this description it is clear that, when Paul says here (in Romans 13), "Whoever loves has fulfilled the Law," it is not at all to be understood as if a person could perfectly satisfy God's Law. For if the apostle says this about the Law as it is considered in its fullest perfection and in its external strictness and severity, then it is certain that such is only being said conditionally: that if there were someone who could love perfectly, he would have fulfilled the Law thereby. But since he is here writing to Christians who are under grace, it follows that he is here speaking about the Law and obedience to it as Christ now lays it upon His believers in the kingdom of grace.

From this we learn, then, that we have nothing to worry about, as if we didn't know how or in what way a person may serve God. For He has clearly revealed in His Word that people are to love God above all things and their neighbor as themselves. And, to be sure, under the Gospel the commandment about love is now even lovelier than it was previously in the Old Testament, since, at that time, they had many more commandments along with this one, especially the manifold Mosaic ceremonies, all of which was an unbearable burden, as Peter calls it (Acts 15). But in the New Testament, now that all Levitical ceremonies and ecclesiastical rites have been abolished by Christ, God requires nothing but faith in Him, and love, as it is written in 1 John 3: "This is His command, that we believe in the name of His Son Jesus Christ and love one another, as He has given us a command."

This love is not feigned, but genuine, as it is written in Romans 12: "Love must not be false." And John says in his First Epistle, chapter 3: "My little children, let us not love with words or with the tongue, but with deeds and truth." But if love is to be with deeds and truth, then it must be active through works. For what sense does it make if someone claims to love his neighbor and then fails to show him any kindness? And as John teaches again: "If anyone has goods of the world and shuts up his heart to [his neighbor], how can the love of God be with him?" Where love is not genuine, it is impossible for faith to be genuine, for faith is powerfully and actively attended by love, and is bound to love with such an inseparable bond that, where there is no love in a man, there is also no faith. The entire argument of the apostle James in chapter 2 pertains to this, where he deals with such mouth-Christians and annihilates their empty boasting: "What good is it," he says, "if someone claims to have faith and yet has no deeds? Can faith (understand—such a dead, imaginary faith, or the empty boast of faith with which neither love nor good works are found) save him? For if a brother or a sister is naked and lacked daily nourishment, and one of you says to them, 'God be with you! Be warm and satisfied!,' but gives them nothing, what good is it?"

This is why the holy apostle depicts for the Christian so frequently and so often that, yes, Christian brotherly love among believers must be sincere, fervent, and without falsehood. Paul says to the Colossians in chapter 3: "Above all, put on love, which is the bond of perfection," that is, through which Christians are united and bound together in a perfect, spiritual body, as with a cord. He explains this again to the Ephesians in chapter 4: "Be diligent to preserve the unity in the Spirit through the bond of peace. One body and one Spirit, as you are also called to one hope of your calling. One Lord, one faith, one Baptism, one God and Father of us all, who is over you all, and through you all, and in you all." Thus all good things spring from Christian love, namely, true, genuine unity, and harmony, as we hear told of the disciples in the early apostolic church in Acts 2 that those who had believed were of one heart and soul. By this harmony and unity, the children of God are known, as we read again in Mat. 5: "Blessed are the peacemakers, for they will be called children of God." And again: "By this it will be known that you are My disciples, if you love one another" (John 13).

It also flows from this that they may come together all the more eagerly in joint prayer, and have all the more benefit from it, since St. Paul admonishes that we should pray for one another—indeed, for all men. For although each Christian can and should also pray on his own, bringing his requests to God, nevertheless the common, joint intercession, including the intercession for others, should not be forgotten.

For these reasons, when Christ prescribed a common form of prayer, He did not forget about love in it, but arranged the prayer in such a way that all Christians pray first and foremost, as He has taught us to pray, "Our Father," and not, "My Father"; "Forgive us our debts," and not, "Forgive me my debts, etc." For wherever the prayer is prayed like this with a unified spirit, it is powerful and effective, according to the promise of the Lord Christ in Matthew 18: "Where two among you on earth agree on what they pray for, it shall be done for them by My Father in heaven."

In this way, the Church of God, through such unified prayer, is strong enough for all her foes, and is protected much more powerfully by such unanimous prayer than she ever could be by shield or weapon.

Such a sincere, brotherly love also results in Christian compassion as one considers the needs and concerns of his neighbor. Then follow soon after the beautiful fruits of love, that one does good to the poor and needy, feeds the hungry, gives drink to the thirsty, clothes the naked, visits the sick, and does other good deeds for them, as Isaiah in chapter 58 and Matthew in chapter 25 recount these things one after another.

Furthermore, love moves a person to excuse his neighbor's faults and weaknesses and to cover up his shame, as it is written in 1 Peter 4: "Above all, have fervent love for one another, for love also covers up a multitude of sins." Understand: it covers up the neighbor's sin, not before God, but before men. It does not broadcast it, as the hypocrites tend to do, who become giddy when they see and experience that other people fall into sin and shame. Love is not so inclined, but hates to see another fall and would rather the sin remain hidden. It also covers up the neighbor's faults, shortcomings and defects, as much as possible and can be done with a good conscience. Yes, love stretches so far and so wide that it even does good to its enemies. The Lord Christ's sermon proclaims the same thing when He says in Matthew 5: "I say to you: Love your enemies. Bless those who curse you. Do good to those who hate you. Pray for those who afflict and persecute you, that you may be children of your Father in heaven. For He causes His sun to rise on the wicked and on the good, and causes it to rain on the righteous and unrighteous. For if you love those who love you, what kind of reward will you have? Do not the tax collectors also do that? And if you only show kindness to your brothers, what are you doing out of the ordinary? Do not the tax collectors do likewise? Therefore you shall be perfect, even as your Father in heaven is perfect."

This is not just "good advice" in the New Testament to be followed according to each one's whim, as if one were not really obliged to love one's enemies, as the Pharisees used to teach. Rather, it is an earnest command of God and a duty that we are bound to perform for all men, both friend and foe. Therefore it was also commanded in the Old Testament in the Law of Moses that, if your enemy's ox or donkey went astray, you should bring it back. And Solomon explains this characteristic of love in Proverbs 25, which St. Paul then sets before Christians as an example in Romans 12: "Do not avenge yourself, my beloved, but leave room for God's wrath. For it is written: 'Vengeance is Mine; I will repay,' says the Lord. So, then, if your enemy is hungry, feed him. If he is thirsty, give him a drink. If you do this, you will heap burning coals upon his head. Let not evil overcome you, but overcome evil with good."

In summary, "Love is longsuffering and kind. Love does not envy. Love does not promote arrogance. It is not puffed up. It does not behave rudely. It is not self-seeking. It does not become bitter. It does not think evil. It does not rejoice when injustice is done, but rejoices when justice is done. It bears all. It trusts all. It hopes all. It endures all. Love never ceases." In this way, the apostle has listed the fruits, virtues and Christian properties of love (1 Cor. 13).

Where love reigns in a Christian congregation, there the whole Table of Duties runs like clockwork. (For we carry out this commandment about love through the Christian Table of Duties and thereby fulfill it.) When a preacher has genuine love for his parishioners and takes care of them with true faithfulness, he will not be able to leave undone his duty to reveal to them the whole counsel of God, that is, to proclaim what is necessary for their eternal salvation. Compelled by love, he will structure everything so that they are pastured with the pure, unadulterated doctrine and instructed with all diligence to eternal life. He will warn them faithfully against temporal and eternal destruction, which is the true nature and character of love. He will admonish them concerning sin and error, for that is the salutary mark of one who truly loves. He will see to it that he does not offend them either with words or with deeds. He will watch over the flock entrusted to him as a good and faithful shepherd who loves the flock entrusted to him. He will be completely diligent to perform rightly the work of a good, evangelical preacher for the eternal benefit of his hearers.

On the other hand, if love also reigns among the hearers, they will, according to the admonition of St. Paul, love and treasure their teachers on account of the office that they perform. They will give to them and provide for them what they owe them according to what is just and right. They will willingly submit to church discipline, and they will strive to this end, that their preachers are not forced to carry out their office with heaviness of heart because of it.

So, too, if Christian love reigns between rulers and subjects, everything in the secular government will run smoothly and properly, so that rulers, compelled and driven by this love, seek, not their own benefit, but the wellbeing of their subjects. They will guard and protect them from all unjust treatment.

The subjects, for their part, will give to their rulers what they owe—honor, fear, obedience, taxes, duties and anything else, and they will be faithful and kind to them.

Husbands will also be compelled by this Christian virtue of love to love their wives sincerely and to be temperate as they live with them. Wives will be submissive to their husbands.

Parents will raise their children in the fear of God and will not fail to discipline them, for this, too, is a fruit of love, as we read in the Proverbs 3: "The father who loves his son disciplines him."

Children will see to it that they honor and love their parents, obey them, and listen to them, and not grieve them as long as they live.

If masters and mistresses are ruled by Christian love, they will not treat their menservants and maidservants like dumb cattle, but will show them proper meekness and gentleness.

Similarly, if menservants, maidservants, hired hands and workers are ruled by a spirit of love, they will follow love's rule by working faithfully. They will not steal anything, for they would not want someone to do that to them if they were in their master's or mistress's position. Through Christian love, the youth also will be a fine example of true, genuine humility (which depends on love, since love is not puffed up – 1 Cor. 13). No less will Christian love compel widows, out of true faith toward God and unfeigned love toward their neighbor, to make prayers and supplication for all men day and night. Thus by means of this explanation of each one's estate and order, it has been thoroughly and specifically demonstrated that in this way love extends generally to all men, and individually to each one in his vocation.

So, then, we have, by the grace of God, brought this interpretation of the entire Table of Duties to an end, having treated in various sermons how each one should live, act, behave, and conduct himself according to his estate and vocation.

We must call upon the eternal, almighty God and Father of our Lord Jesus Christ, that this explanation may prove useful to many people and produce fruit, so that preachers may set an example for the churches of God with salutary teaching and holy living; that their hearers may receive the preached word with faith and follow it obediently; that rulers may wield justice and righteousness; and that their subjects may be obedient; that husbands and wives may be fully and faithfully committed and united to each other; that parents may guide their children in the discipline and instruction of the Lord, and that children may also gladly follow their lead; also that masters and mistresses, young and old, and everyone in general may remember his lesson and put it into practice, and thus that a peaceful life on earth may be fostered in every estate, so that kindness and faithfulness may meet one another, righteousness and peace kiss each other (Psa. 85), faithfulness may grow on earth and righteousness appear from heaven; and that we may in this way live out the remainder of this vain, passing life in this world in true harmony with one another, until the distinction between estates is abolished and we enjoy eternal fellowship in perfect, eternal righteousness and holiness with God and the Lord Jesus Christ, together with the Holy Spirit, and, together with the holy, elect angels, praise, honor and glorify Him forever and ever. Amen.

Here ends the explanation of the Table of Duties.

Scriptural Index

Old Testament

Genesis
1 - 87
2 - 87
3 - 75
6 - 29
9 - 97, 101, 104
17 - 120
22 - 96, 101, 140
24 - 97, 101
27 - 96
28 - 97
29 - 113
31 - 123
41 - 130
47 - 98

Exodus
1 - 58
18 - 95
21 - 38, 103
22 - 38, 52
23 - 42, 47

Leviticus
19 - 130
25 - 122

Numbers
16 - 28
18 - 31
21 - 68

Deuteronomy
6 - 85
14 - 31
16 - 43
17 - 40
18 - 31
21 - 103
23 - 123
24 - 121
26 - 31

Judges
9 - 56, 104

Ruth
2 - 98
3 - 144

1 Samuel
3 - 87
4 - 87
8 - 60
9 - 102
10 - 102
14 - 90, 109
16 - 102
17 - 102
20 - 90, 96
22 - 58, 98, 113
25 - 109
30 - 126

2 Samuel
4 - 56

15 - 62
16 - 53
17 - 63
18 - 56, 63, 113
21 - 63

1 Kings
17 - 142

2 Kings
2 - 28
5 - 33, 110
12 - 57
17 - 57

Esther
2 - 57, 63

Job
13 - 108
29 - 38, 41, 43, 54
32 - 131
39 - 84

Psalm
1 - 12
24 - 64
34 - 140
68 - 140
78 - 85
82 - 38, 45
85 - 157
101 - 42, 46
103 - 81, 114
113 - 140
119 - 134
123 - 110
127 - 80
147 - 84

Proverbs
1 - 135
5 - 74
6 - 77, 91
10 - 91
13 - 134
16 - 41, 43
17 - 105
19 - 41, 91, 103
20 - 42, 43, 91, 104
21 - 64
23 - 96
24 - 56
25 - 154
26 - 56
28 - 91
29 - 88
30 - 103, 104
31 - 77, 78, 122

Ecclesiastes
5 - 12
12 - 136

Isaiah
1 - 43, 72, 141
5 - 47
8 - 48
30 - 27
43 - 114
46 - 29, 136
49 - 81
55 - 107
57 - 140
58:1 - 16, 153

Jeremiah
6 - 30
22 - 44
23 - 13, 17
44 - 30

Lamentations
5 - 125

Ezekiel
33 - 16, 28

Daniel
2 - 130
3 - 59
6 - 59
12 - 22

Micah
2 - 27

Zechariah
7 - 141

Malachai
1 - 108
2 - 12, 72

Apocrypha
Sirach
3 - 98, 104, 101
4 - 41, 101, 141
6 - 26
7 - 32, 100, 120
8 - 132
10 - 42, 52
13 - 134
19 - 131
20 - 44
25 - 76, 78
30 - 87, 88
32 - 132
33 - 124, 127
35 - 47, 72, 122, 141, 146
39 - 15

Tobit
4 - 86

Wisdom of Solomon
2 - 135
3 - 45
4 - 133, 134
6 - 44
8 - 137

New Testament
Matthew
1 - 143
3:17 - 11
5 - 18, 152, 154
7 - 1, 126
8 - 39, 111
10 - 33, 34
12 - 137
15 - 94, 114
16 - 11
17 - 60
18 - 19, 64, 80, 89, 111, 112
20 - 108
22 - 59, 60
23 - 19
25 - 153
26 - 57

Mark
10 - 80

Luke
2 - 146
3 - 39
6 - 140
7 - 20, 142
10 - 11, 28, 113
12 - 117
17 - 121

John
4 - 120
7 - 38, 113
12 - 113
13 - 152
15 - 22
16 - 29
19 - 98
20 - 12

Acts
2 - 152
5 - 58, 112
7 - 29, 143
10 - 120
15 - 150
18 - 14
20 - 15, 18

Romans
1 - 13
2 - 19
6 - 84
12 - 150, 154
13 - 37, 51, 149
14 - 5

1 Corinthians
1 - 13
3 - 14
4 - 26
7 - 108, 144
9 - 14, 32
13 - 154, 156
15 - 134

2 Corinthians
2 - 81
5 - 12

Galatians
3 - 108
4 - 26, 27
5 - 17, 74
6 - 33, 34

Ephesians
4 - 133, 152
6 - 79, 93, 107, 119
6:4 - 79

Colossians
3 - 114, 152
3:21 - 79

1 Thessalonians
2 - 11
4 - 29
5 - 25

1 Timothy
2 - 63, 68, 75
3 - 9, 2, 68
4 - 15 , 21

5 - 26, 82, 98, 139
6 - 117

2 Timothy
2 - 16, 22
4 - 13, 23

Titus
1 - 9
2 - 116
3 - 57, 83

Hebrews
11 - 5, 38
13 - 28, 70, 74

James
2 - 152

1 Peter
4 - 153
5 - 23, 129

2 Peter
1 - 10
2 - 33, 39, 52, 58
3 - 11

1 John
2 - 133, 149
3 - 151

Revelation
3 - 22
17 - 33
18 - 33

www.ingramcontent.com/pod-product-compliance
Lightning Source LLC
LaVergne TN
LVHW051602070426
835507LV00021B/2722